Wildflowers of the Outer Banks

The Dunes of Dare Garden Club
Wildflower Identification Committee

Sarah T. Barber

Margaret M. Held

Ina B. Kuralt

Helen Hill Miller

Bernice Mulford

Marie-Louise Peterson

Gertrude Rogallo

Virginia F. Ross

Mary N. Torrey

Bertha M. Willett

Wildflowers of the Outer Banks

Kitty Hawk to Hatteras

The Dunes of Dare Garden Club

Illustrated by Jane Sutton

The University of North Carolina Press *Chapel Hill*

© 1980 The University of North Carolina Press
All rights reserved
Manufactured in the United States of America
ISBN 0-8078-4060-2
Library of Congress Catalog Card Number 79-18927

Library of Congress Cataloging in Publication Data
Dunes of Dare Garden Club. Wildflower Identification
  Committee.
  Wildflowers of the Outer Banks.

  Bibliography: p.
  Includes index.
  1. Wild flowers—North Carolina—Outer Banks—
Identification. I. Title.
QK178.D86 1980   582'.13'097561   79-18927
ISBN 0-8078-4060-2

Contents

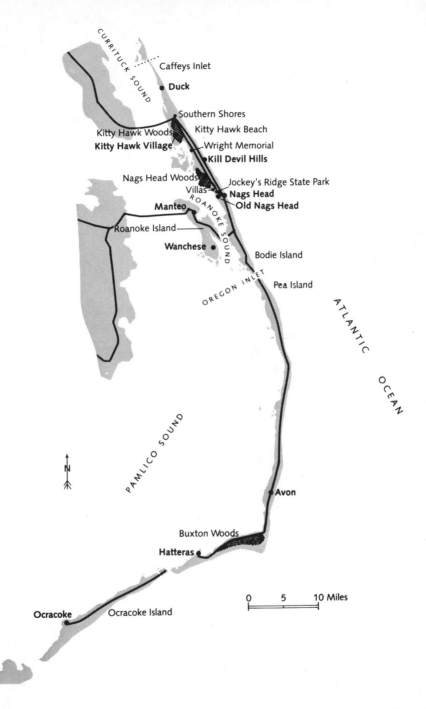

CURRITUCK SOUND

Caffeys Inlet

● **Duck**

●Southern Shores

Kitty Hawk Woods   Kitty Hawk Beach

Kitty Hawk Village   Wright Memorial

● **Kill Devil Hills**

Nags Head Woods   Jockey's Ridge State Park

Villas   ● **Nags Head**

Manteo ●   Old Nags Head

Roanoke Island

ROANOKE SOUND

Wanchese ●   Bodie Island

Pea Island

OREGON INLET

ATLANTIC OCEAN

PAMLICO SOUND

N

● **Avon**

Buxton Woods

Hatteras ●

0   5   10 Miles

Ocracoke ●   Ocracoke Island

Acknowledgments

Jane Sutton, the illustrator who drew the flora for this book, has served as a naturalist with Blue Ridge Parkway, Cape Hatteras National Seashore, and Hanging Rock State Park. The accuracy of both the descriptions and the illustrations was verified by Clay L. Gifford, a naturalist serving as resource management specialist for the Cape Hatteras National Seashore.

Botanist Dr. Lytton J. Musselman, assistant professor of biological science and curator of the herbarium, Old Dominion University, Norfolk, Virginia, verified pressed specimens before their placement in the Cape Hatteras National Seashore Herbarium.

Special thanks are due to Dr. James W. Hardin, professor of botany and curator of the herbarium, North Carolina State University, Raleigh, for permission to use material from his contribution to *Endangered and Threatened Plants and Animals of North Carolina*, for editing and correcting the glossary, and for his general encouragement over the years. Through his patronage, pressed specimens of the committee's new finds are being placed in the North Carolina State University Herbarium.

The ever patient Hilda Livingston, educational coordinator, North Carolina Marine Resources Center, cheerfully gave hours of her time to the skilled preparation of reproductions of the drawings for the initial submission of the manuscript to the publisher.

Lynanne B. Wescott, business manager of the Eastern National Park and Monument Association, was a source of experienced advice on format and distribution.

Dunes of Dare Garden Club member Kay Kenan devoted many hours to typing and retyping versions of the text and the meticulously accurate listings that follow it.

Introduction

Wildflowers of the Outer Banks: Kitty Hawk to Hatteras had its start five years ago when a group of amateur botanists, under the leadership of Marie-Louise Peterson, organized the Wildflower Identification Committee of the Dunes of Dare Garden Club. Each member had found the Outer Banks of North Carolina and chosen to become a part of the permanent residential community there. The discovery of beautiful wildflowers and shrubs, thriving in the unique growing conditions of the area, was a delightful surprise. The goals of the committee were to identify these plants and to share this knowledge with others.

Field trips in Dare County were scheduled monthly during the growing season. New specimens were discovered, some rare and some on the endangered species list. Color slides recorded more than 100 plants; these slides are now in active use for slide shows.

The Cape Hatteras National Seashore Herbarium was inventoried, and new specimens, as they were discovered, were pressed and added to the herbarium list. This list then aided the committee in classifying plants that had previously been identified by observation only. Since members were now doing professional work for which they lacked training, a college-level botany course was organized. Taught by botanist-artist Jane Sutton, this course enabled the committee to classify plants in less time and with greater accuracy. So when asked why it did not write a book, the committee was ready to accept the challenge.

The Outer Banks Area

The Outer Banks is a series of long, narrow sandbars and islands which run in a north-south direction from the Virginia–North Carolina state line to Cape Hatteras, then turn sharply southwest to rejoin the mainland shore above Cape Fear. Although the distance from the state line to the southern tip of Ocracoke Island is some ninety miles, the Banks are rarely more than a mile and a half wide. Roanoke Island is connected to the Banks by a man-made causeway at South Nags Head; on its northeastern tip, the men and women sent out by Sir Walter Raleigh in 1587 attempted to plant the first permanent English settlement in America. At the site, the Garden Club of North Carolina has memorialized the pioneers of the Lost Colony in the Elizabethan Gardens—twelve and a half landscaped and cultivated acres. Wildflowers abound in other sections of the island.

The map at the front of the book shows this geography and calls attention to a number of places where specimens of the flowers shown on the following pages are likely to be found.

What Grows Where—and Why

To exist on the Outer Banks, plants require exceptional hardiness and adaptability.
They must endure frequent flooding from an aroused ocean or from wind-driven sound waters, and wide changes of temperature and wind speed that may occur in minutes as weather fronts pass through. On the ocean side of the Banks, the few existing plants must resist a coating of salt and violently driven sand that covers and uncovers, quickly dries out, and absorbs and reflects scorching heat in the extreme summer temperatures.

Because of varying degrees of adaptability to the extreme conditions, different kinds of plant growth occur in distinct zones parallel to the beach. Three zones and their accompanying characteristic plants are easily recognized: (1) the frontal zone (including primary and secondary dunes) along the ocean shore, where sea oats, American beach grass, and seaside elder hold their own; (2) the shrub zone, where, protected from salt concentration and harsh winds by the secondary dune (the natural or man-made dune landward from the primary dune) wax myrtle, bayberry, groundsel-tree, salt-meadow cordgrass, persimmon, and a variety of asters and low-growing plants occur; (3) the woodland zone, which supports a wide range of trees —pine, holly, live oak, sweet-gum, dogwood—and flowers—lady's slipper, partridge berry, lizard's tail, false foxglove—as well as a number of aquatic species in the woodland ponds.

Adaptations required for survival are easily recognized. Many plants on the ocean side are small and thick, dwarfed by the force of the sand, salt, wind, and water to which they are constantly subjected. Plants that do well are apt to have thick, glossy, hairy, or sometimes succulent leaves for retaining and holding water; complex root systems for security in the shifting sands and for capturing moisture as quickly as possible before it evaporates or seeps through the porous sand; and special mechanisms to expel salt. Most of these plants have twice the growing season of plants in the Piedmont region of the state.

Observers who begin their wildflower explorations on the ocean side are likely to find the prickly pear or beach evening primrose in May or June, sea oats in July or August, and seaside goldenrod or groundsel-tree in September or October. Those who start in the woods or marshy spots are likely to find Carolina ipecac or yellow jessamine in April; blue-eyed grass, coral honeysuckle, pickerelweed, or Venus' looking glass in May or June; orange milkweed, mallow, and meadow beauty in July or August; and cardinal flowers, mistflowers, and asters in September or October.

One further group of plants is sure to be noticed: the escapees from cultivated gardens. Borne by the persistent winds, their seeds have been sown far and wide, and then firmly established in wild areas. Coreopsis, gaillardia, and yucca are plentiful, and the roadsides of Kitty Hawk Village are brilliant in spring and summer with annual phlox in many colors.

The unusual conditions on the Banks give special interest to the study of its flowers, whether by Bankers who have lived here all their lives, by visitors coming for the first time, by novices receiving their first botany lessons as they roam, or by specialists who are professionals in the field. For all who look, new discoveries are waiting.

About the Text

In its own explorations, the committee not only has identified 500 species overall but has found 96 not previously known to exist in Dare County and 5 whose presence was hitherto unknown in North Carolina. In choosing the 122 varieties to be illustrated and described in this book the committee selected, in addition to a few that are uncommon or of special interest, those that are most noticeable when in bloom and those most inquired about by visitors.

For quick reference, the sections of the text separate flowers according to color. Each listing includes first the common name of the plant, followed by the scientific and the English family names. The order of the plants within each section was adopted for artistic reasons.

Within a species, plants vary considerably in appearance and size, from dwarfs to giants. The illustrations show *average* sizes. Since most of the drawings were reduced according to space requirements, a line scale is provided with each drawing.

The descriptions of the plants also include notes on their cultivation and propagation and the habitats in which they are likely to do well; briefer notes cite uses that may have been made of them in the past for medicine, food, or fiber. The early settlers learned many things from the Indians, one of which was undoubtedly the use of Hercules'-club as a toothache remedy. They chewed the twigs and leaves, which contain a substance similar to oil of lemon found in modern-day remedies, into a wad which was packed around the aching tooth. Additional temporary solace was furnished by other druglike properties of the "toothache bush." The Indians from the area, as well as the settlers, made a brew from yaupon and roasted or boiled the root of groundnut for a potato substitute. Before duplicating such practices, be sure to obtain exact information. Some plants are POISONOUS:

when boiled, fresh young leaves of pokeweed make excellent spring greens, but more mature foliage acts as a powerful cathartic!

At the back of the book there is a complete list of pressed specimens found in the herbarium at the National Park Service Headquarters, Cape Hatteras National Seashore, Roanoke Island, which is open during all seasons. Recent additions, which were identified and submitted by the committee, include many specimens that were observed for the first time in the county and the state; the contents of the herbarium, however, do not represent all of the plants known to exist in Dare County. In the herbarium list, the flowers are grouped by families in numerical order, as found in the *Manual of the Vascular Flora of the Carolinas*, by Albert E. Radford, Henry E. Ahles, and C. Ritchie Bell.

A list of useful reference works, a glossary, and an index of the varieties covered in the text will also be found at the end of the book.

Because of the fragile ecology of the Outer Banks the uprooting of plants or picking of flowers is discouraged; plants are needed for stabilizing and preserving the land. Moreover, some plants are in special need of protection. The North Carolina State Museum of Natural History issues a list of threatened or endangered species in the state, *Endangered and Threatened Plants and Animals of North Carolina*, by John E. Cooper, Sarah S. Robinson and John Funderberg, which includes peripheral species that are rare in North Carolina, the outer limit of their ranges (see page 155 for a further discussion of rare and endangered species). The new plant legislation passed in the 1979 North Carolina General Assembly and effective 1 July 1980 revises the list of plants protected by state law and replaces the conservation list of the Garden Club of North Carolina. None of the plants described in this text is included in the new state list.

In offering this result of several years of exploration, the Wildflower Identification Committee of the Dunes of Dare Garden Club wishes, both to visitors to the Outer

Banks and to residents bent
on increasing their familiarity
with their surroundings, the
same pleasure of discovery and
identification that its members have themselves enjoyed.

How to Use This Book

Each description contains most or all of these elements.

Common name

Scientific name

Author

Northern Bedstraw
Galium boreale L.
Madder

English family name

Classification

Perennial or annual herb, newly found in area, 1 to 2½ feet tall. Stem erect, rather stiff, sharply 4 angled and smooth. Leaves narrow, whorled. Flower bright white. Red to brownish pink dye made from roots may be used when a pure vegetable dye is desired, especially for wool. Dry, sandy roadsides. Chicahauk. Southern Shores. Mid-May.

Size

Stem

Leaves

Flowers

Uses and lore

Habitat

Likely sites

Season

Scale
(Drawings are reduced. Line scale is equal to one inch of actual size.)

Section I

White or Cream-Colored Flowers

Duck Potato, Arrowhead
Sagittaria falcata Pursh
Water-Plantain

Native aquatic perennial herb, up to 4 feet tall. Flowers white, along a tall, leafless stalk. Mature tubers were boiled, peeled, and eaten hot or in cold "Duck Potato Salad" by Indians and colonists. May have been served as a delicacy with freshly caught fish. Marsh areas. Duck Road north end. June–September.

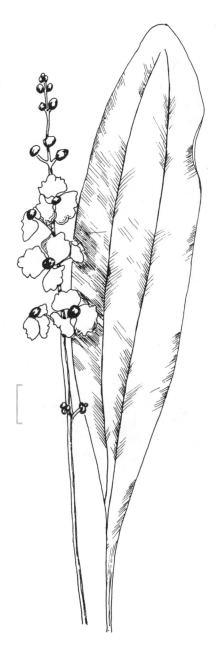

White Fringed-Orchid
Habenaria blephariglottis (Willd.) Hooker
Orchis

Herb, 2 to 3 feet tall, found in large colonies in wet roadsides and ditches. Root fleshy. Flowers white and showy, tempting to pick. Wanchese Road. Mid-August.

Nodding, Fragrant, or Autumn Ladies' Tresses
Spiranthes cernua var. *odorata* (Nuttall) Correll
Orchis

Herb, 8 to 18 inches tall from
tuberous roots; often standing
in water. Flowers, creamy to
greenish white, form a dense
spiral along the single spike;
fragrance is likened to a mix-
ture of jasmine and vanilla.
Wet roadsides, ditches. Duck
Road north end; Wanchese
Road. Early October.

Spotted Water Hemlock
Cicuta maculata L.
Parsley

Perennial herb, 2 to 5 feet
tall; roots tuberous and finger-
like, resembling sweet pota-
toes. Stem stout, often purple, mottled. Leaves large,
alternate, pinnately divided,
with leaflets to 7 inches long
and 2½ inches wide. Flowers
white, in compound flat-
topped clusters; the pleasant
parsniplike fragrance is de-
ceiving, for it should not be
confused with the plant used
as herb or medicine. This
plant is highly POISONOUS
to humans and livestock if
eaten. Socrates was poisoned
by the closely related *Conium
maculatum*, poison hemlock,
a native of the Old World and
also a weed in this country.
Along sounds, lagoons, low
roadsides; near marshes.
Throughout the area. May–
August.

Queen Anne's Lace, Wild Carrot
Daucus carota L.
Parsley

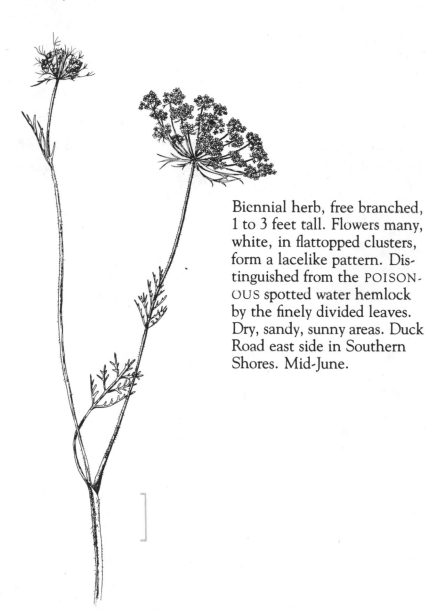

Biennial herb, free branched, 1 to 3 feet tall. Flowers many, white, in flattopped clusters, form a lacelike pattern. Distinguished from the POISONOUS spotted water hemlock by the finely divided leaves. Dry, sandy, sunny areas. Duck Road east side in Southern Shores. Mid-June.

Hyssop-Leaved Thoroughwort
Eupatorium hyssopifolium L.
Aster

Perennial herb, erect, rather bushy, 1 to 2 feet tall. Flowers white. Leaves narrow in whorls of 4 or more. One of many species of thoroughwort in this area. Dry, sandy, sunny roadsides. Duck Road to Hatteras. July–several months later.

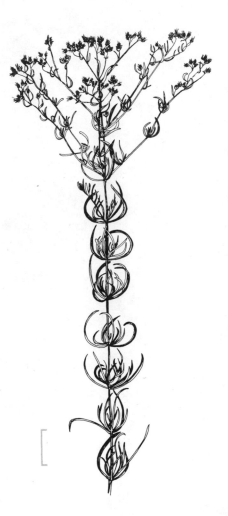

Round-Leaved Thoroughwort
Eupatorium rotundifolium L.
Aster

Perennial herb, up to 4 feet
tall. Stem stiff, erect. Leaves
opposite, some roundish.
Flowers white. Dry to peaty,
acid marsh soil. Common.
Ocean Acres, Kill Devil Hills;
east of Duck Road. June.

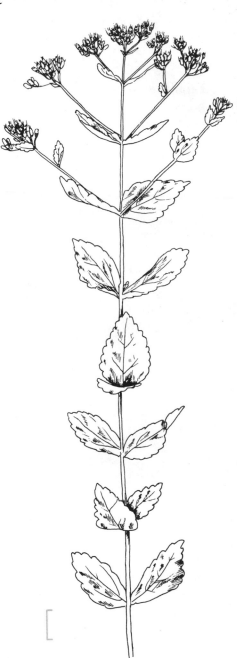

White Bay, Sweet Bay
Magnolia virginiana L.
Magnolia

Small semievergreen tree, up to 50 feet tall. Leaves alternate, oblong, dark green above and whitish beneath. Flowers creamy white, cup shaped. Fruit cluster 2 inches long with flat red seeds. Root bark was a substitute for quinine as a treatment for malaria in colonial times. Bays, lagoons, and sound borders. Throughout the area. April–June, July–October.

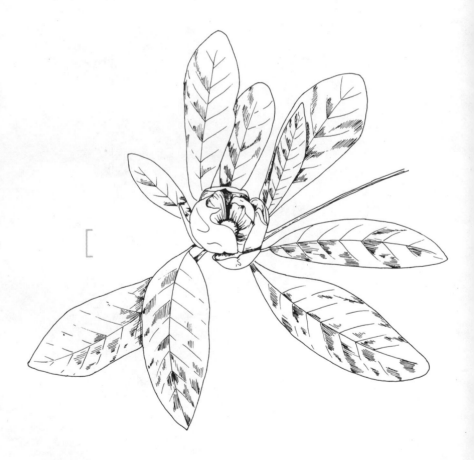

Flowering Dogwood
Cornus florida L.
Dogwood

Small tree, 10 to 40 feet tall, with opposite leaves. Flowers small and yellow, surrounded by 4 large white conspicuous bracts appearing before full leaf development. Red fruit (see small sketch) provides food for migratory birds through December. Also known as "spindle tree," its fine hard wood was imported from the New World by England for the manufacture of spindles used in weaving. Understory pine and deciduous woods. Throughout wooded sections of area. Late March–April, September–December.

Groundsel-Tree, Sea-Myrtle, Salt Myrtle
Baccharis halimifolia L.
Aster

Native shrub, 6 to 8 feet tall, with resinous, wedge-shaped, coarsely toothed leaves. Male and female plants: male flowers (see small sketch) creamy white; female flowers white, most conspicuous in fruit (see large sketch). Good for salt wind barrier and screening. Useful for dune erosion control or in any local natural seacoast garden. Thickets and borders of marshes. Southern Shores; Bodie Island. October.

Coast Pepperbush, White Alder
Clethra alnifolia L.
White Alder

Native shrub, many
branched, 3 to 9 feet tall.
Leaves alternate, finely
toothed toward tip. Flowers
white (enlarged sketch),
densely clustered along stem;
fragrance spicy. Seed pods
form in fall (shown separate-
ly). Moist, sunny shrub areas.
Duck Village road to sound.
Mid-August.

Rabbit Tobacco
Gnaphalium obtusifolium L.
Aster

Herb, annual or biennial,
woolly, 1 to 4 feet tall. Flowers grayish white. Dried leaves
are used by American children as play-store tobacco;
leaves and stems were used to
stuff pillows and mattresses.
The plant is attractive in dried
arrangements. Dry, sandy,
sunny, open areas. Within
200 feet of ocean throughout the Banks. August–
winter.

Ox-eye Daisy, White Daisy
Chrysanthemum leucanthemum L.
Aster

Native herb of Europe and
Asia, usually perennial in this
area, 1 to 2 feet tall. Stem
erect. Ray flowers white, disc
flowers yellow in a head. Said
to have been used medicinally
as tea for whooping cough and
asthma. Open, sunny, sandy
lots. Kitty Hawk Beach between Route 158 and Route
158 bypass. June.

Common Yarrow, Milfoil
Achillea millefolium L.
Aster

Perennial herb, naturalized
from Europe, 1 to 3 feet tall.
Stem erect. Leaves finely
pinnately dissected. Used
medicinally to control bleeding, reduce inflammation in
wounds, and relieve toothache. White, many-flowered
head. Roadsides, open lots.
Grows within 20 feet of
ocean. June.

Northern Bedstraw
Galium boreale L.
Madder

Perennial or annual herb,
newly found in area, 1 to 2½
feet tall. Stem erect, rather
stiff, sharply 4 angled and
smooth. Leaves narrow,
whorled. Flower bright white.
Red to brownish pink dye
made from roots may be used
when a pure vegetable dye is
desired, especially for wool.
Dry, sandy roadsides. Chicahauk, Southern Shores.
Mid-May.

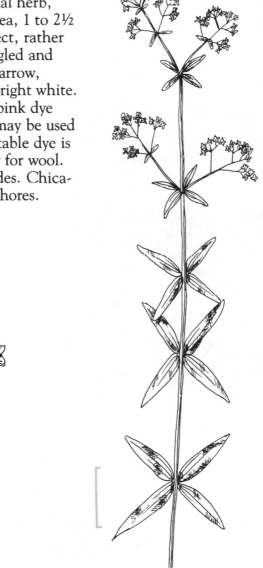

Climbing Hydrangea
Decumaria barbara L.
Saxifrage

High-climbing woody vine, clings to tree trunk and appears to be part of the tree. Leaves opposite, thick, dark green. Flowers white, profuse and fragrant, mistlike in rounded clusters. Sunny, cleared woody areas. Juniper Lane, Southern Shores. Late May–early June.

Elderberry
Sambucus canadensis L.
Honeysuckle

Shrublike herb, 3 to 10 feet tall. Leaves opposite, pinnately divided. Stem hollow, made into flutes and whistles by children, but is POISONOUS. Flowers white, fragrant, in broad, flattopped clusters. Berries used for jelly, ink, dye, and wine. Wet, sunny sound banks. Kitty Hawk sand road. Mid-May.

Black Cherry
Prunus serotina Ehrh.
Rose

Large native tree moderately resistant to salt spray, thrives in poor soil but survives only briefly in competition for sunlight; useful in landscaping. Bark smooth, dark; when young, satiny reddish brown with horizontal markings; when mature, small scaly plates, edges slightly upraised. Leaves alternate, hairy underneath along midrib—a distinctive feature. Flowers white. Fruit (see small sketch) is choice food for a variety of birds. Sunny roadsides near sounds. Kitty Hawk Bay Road. Mid-April, early June.

Juneberry, Serviceberry, Shadbush
Amelanchier canadensis (L.) Medicus
Rose

Native shrub or tree, up to 20 feet tall. Bark brownish red. Leaves alternate, still folded when clouds of white flowers appear in early spring. Fruit edible, reddish purple, sweet- ish, applelike, ripe in early April. Thin woods, thickets, low ground. Kill Devil Hills, area north of Wright Memorial; Bodie Island. Mid-March.

Spotted Pipsissewa
Chimaphila maculata (L.) Pursh
Heath

Perennial evergreen, up to
10 inches tall. Leaves deeply
toothed, variegated, tapered
to apex. Flowers nodding,
creamy white, fragrant, often
seen on same plant with seeds.
Leaves and fruit used for
tonic. Pine woods. Eastern
side of hill in Nags Head
Woods; Kill Devil Hills. Early
June.

Partridge Berry
Mitchella repens L.
Madder

Perennial, evergreen and
prostrate. Leaves dark green,
opposite and leathery. Flowers white, waxy, fragrant,
borne in pairs united at base.
Berry red and aromatic, provides food for birds. Tea made
from plant is a remedy for in-
somnia and excess water re-
tention. Woods throughout
area. Mid-May, June.

Lizard's Tail
Saururus cernuus L.
Lizard's Tail

Perennial herb, usually
aquatic, spreads by rhizomes
into large colonies. Stem 1 to
3 feet. Leaves alternate, large,
heart shaped, pointed and
dark green. Flowers white,
minute, on elongated spike
drooping at top of plant.
Banks of fresh ponds. Kitty
Hawk Woods; Nags Head
Woods. June–end of summer.

Button Bush
Cephalanthus occidentalis L.
Madder

Perennial shrub, 3 to 5 feet tall. Leaves opposite or whorled. Flowers in a round white ball that resembles a pincushion; fragrance jasminelike, attractive to bees. Seed ball (see small sketch) forms in the fall. According to tradition, the bark was chewed by the Indians to relieve toothache, boiled for fevers, and brewed as a tea to induce vomiting. Along sounds and wet roadsides. Kitty Hawk Village Road. July.

Spoonleaf Yucca, Bear Grass
Yucca filamentosa L.
Lily

Evergreen, salt resistant, useful in dune control. Stem
erect. Leaves mostly basal,
narrow, pointed, thick and
leathery, with curly threads
along the edge. Flowers
creamy white, bell shaped,
in large branched clusters;
edible. To prepare for eating,
remove bees, dip bloom in
beaten egg, dust with flour, fry
in fat being careful not to
burn; serve hot. Thrives in
the open and in woods
throughout the area. May–
June.

Section II   Yellow Flowers

Seaside Goldenrod
Solidago sempervirens var. *mexicana* (L.) Fernald
Aster

Perennial herb, stocky, rarely
branched, may grow to height
of 8 feet. Stem erect. Lower
leaves 8 to 12 inches long; upper leaves smaller, lancelike
and pointed. Flowers, yellow
in elongated clusters, attract
thousands of Monarch butterflies during their migratory
flights southward. It multi-
plies rapidly and recommends
itself to seashore gardeners.
Brackish marshes, saline
sands, frontal dunes. Late
August–frost.

Lance-Leaved Goldenrod
Solidago graminifolia (L.) Salisbury
Aster

Perennial herb, rather rare. 1 to 8 feet tall. Stem erect. Flower heads yellow in corymbs; used by early settlers for yellow dye. Fresh plant was used medicinally by Indians. Damp, sandy soil. Duck Road; near sounds, roadsides. September.

Bush Goldenrod
Solidago microcephala (Greene) Bush
Aster

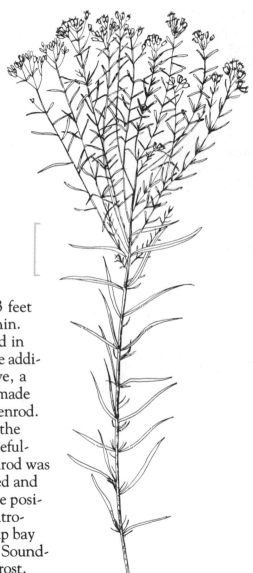

Perennial herb, 1½ to 3 feet
tall. Leaves long and thin.
Flower heads yellow and in
small corymbs. With the addition of alum as a fixative, a
fine yellow dye can be made
from all species of goldenrod.
Greatly appreciated by the
early colonists for its useful-
ness and beauty, goldenrod was
enthusiastically accepted and
elevated to a respectable posi-
tion in gardens when introduced in England. Damp bay
areas. Southern Shores Sound-
side. Late September–frost.

Lance-Leaved Coreopsis
Coreopsis lanceolata L.
Aster

Perennial herb, rises in large
clumps to a height of 1 to 1½
feet; easily grown, reseeds
rapidly. Stems erect. Leaves
deeply lobed, opposite. Rays
of flower brilliant yellow. The
sun-loving blooms follow the
path of the sun from east to
west. Dry, sandy soil. Large
colonies in Kill Devil Hills
between Route 158 and Route
158 bypass. May.

Calliopsis
Coreopsis basalis (Dietrich) Blake
Aster

Winter annual, 1 to 2 feet
tall. Stem erect. Leaves opposite, deeply lobed. Rays
yellow with red stain at
base. Probably introduced.
Dry, sandy soil. Atlantic
Boulevard in Southern
Shores; Old Nags Head Road.
May–June.

Sea Ox-eye
Borrichia frutescens (L.) DC.
Aster

Shrub, 1 to 2½ feet tall, often freely branched, produces extensive colonies from underground rhizomes. Stem erect. Leaves opposite, oblong. Yellow ray and disk flowers in a large, single head. It is characteristic of brackish marshes where low grounds are subject to overflow from sounds. Wet roadsides. Bodie Island; Wanchese Road; Hatteras. Mid-August.

False Dandelion, Fireweed

Pyrrhopappus carolinianus (Walter) DC.

Aster

Biennial herb, up to 1½ feet
tall. Stem erect, leafy. Basal
leaves dandelionlike. Ray
flowers yellow in large head;
anthers black. Roadsides
throughout the area. April–
sporadically later.

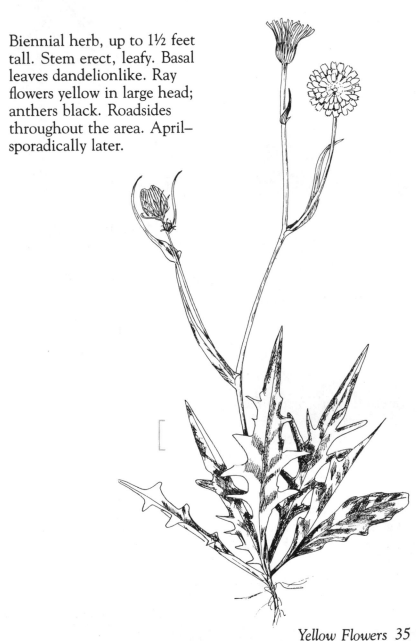

Common Autumn Sneezeweed
Helenium autumnale L.
Aster

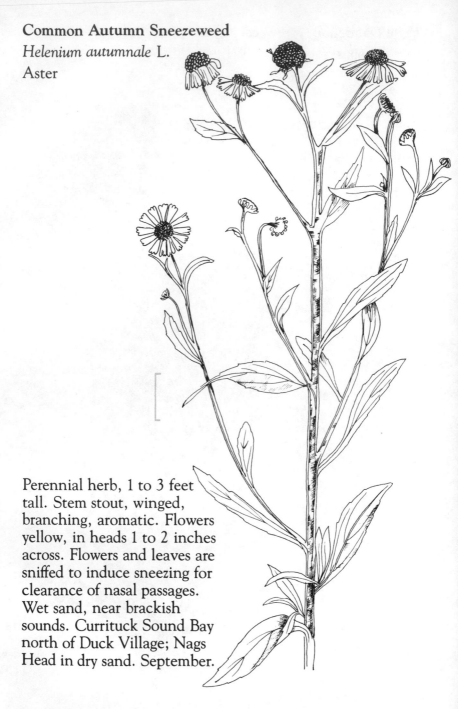

Perennial herb, 1 to 3 feet tall. Stem stout, winged, branching, aromatic. Flowers yellow, in heads 1 to 2 inches across. Flowers and leaves are sniffed to induce sneezing for clearance of nasal passages. Wet sand, near brackish sounds. Currituck Sound Bay north of Duck Village; Nags Head in dry sand. September.

Duney Aster, Decumbent Golden Aster
Heterotheca gossypina (Michaux) Shinners
Aster

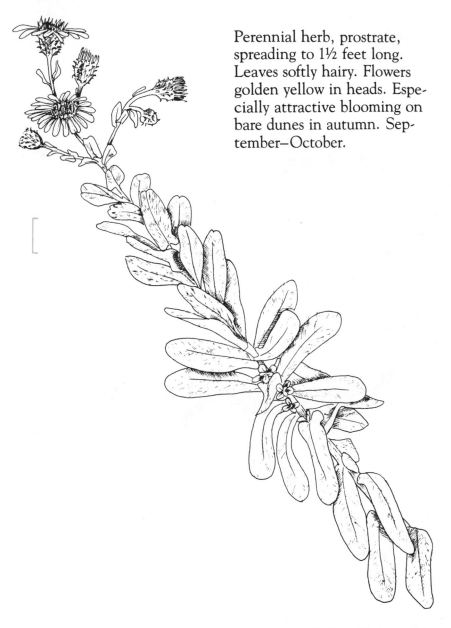

Perennial herb, prostrate, spreading to 1½ feet long. Leaves softly hairy. Flowers golden yellow in heads. Especially attractive blooming on bare dunes in autumn. September–October.

Slender or Yellow Fumewort
Corydalis micrantha ssp. *australis* (Chapm.) Ownbey
Fumitory

Annual or biennial herb, 10
to 12 inches tall; native to
central United States, it was
introduced south of this area
and spread northward. Flowers tubular, yellow, in erect
clusters. Roadsides. Southern
Shores. Mid-March.

Partridge Pea
Cassia fasciculata Michaux
Bean

Annual herb, stem 1 to 1½
feet tall. Leaves alternate,
pinnately divided, sensitive to
touch. Flower has 5 large yellow petals. Seed pod is bean-
like and persists through the
winter. Roadsides both dry
and damp. Nags Head; Duck
Road north end. September.

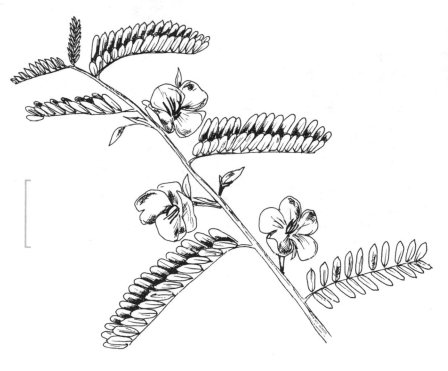

Prickly Pear, Cactus, Indian Fig
Opuntia drummondii Graham
Cactus

Perennial succulent, low,
prostrate, with flat-jointed
pads. Leaves small, scalelike,
appear briefly. Spines slender
and can inflict painful
wounds. Flower yellow, 2 to 3
inches across, opens in sun-
shine 2 or more days. Fruit
purplish red, pear shaped, 1½
inches long; edible only after
tiny spines are removed. To
remove spines, peel or rub
with cloth, or as Indians did,
scrub pear with a handful of
grass. Peripheral species, considered endangered in North
Carolina. Sandy, sunny, dry
dunes. Throughout the area.
May–June, October.

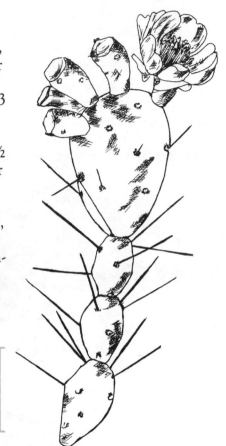

Beach Heather, Woolly Hudsonia
Hudsonia tomentosa Nuttall
Rockrose

Perennial, shrublike, matted, up to 12 inches tall. Leaves scalelike and overlapping. Flowers yellow (see enlarged sketch); blooming period short. Excellent sand binder. Northern native and very rare in the Carolinas. Considered endangered in North Carolina. Dry dunes, edge of woods. Nags Head; Kill Devil Hills near Nags Head Woods. Middle of May.

St. Andrew's Cross
Hypericum hypericoides (L.) Crantz
St. John's-wort

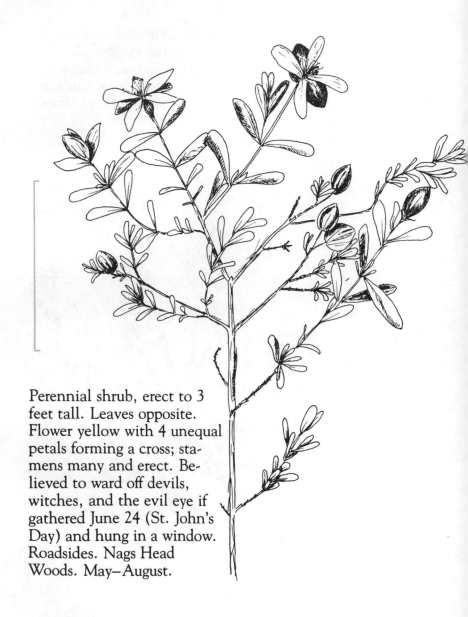

Perennial shrub, erect to 3
feet tall. Leaves opposite.
Flower yellow with 4 unequal
petals forming a cross; stamens many and erect. Be-
lieved to ward off devils,
witches, and the evil eye if
gathered June 24 (St. John's
Day) and hung in a window.
Roadsides. Nags Head
Woods. May–August.

Pineweed, Orange Grass
Hypericum gentianoides (L.) BSP.
St. John's-wort

Annual herb, erect, 4 to 18 inches tall. Leaves ascending and minute, opposite. Flowers 5 petaled, with many erect stamens. Produces gray dye if picked in July; greenish yellow if picked in August. Roadsides. Duck Road; First Flight Village, Kill Devil Hills. July–end of summer.

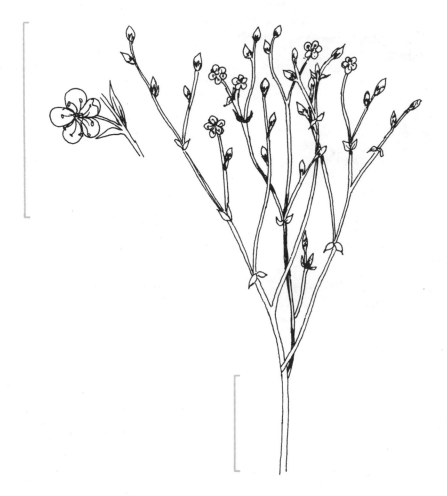

Wild Radish
Raphanus raphanistrum L.
Mustard

Annual, coarse winter herb,
1 to 2½ feet tall, blooms
sporadically throughout 3
seasons. Flower with 4 yellow
distinctly veined petals. Early
green leaves edible—usually
boiled. Dry roadsides.
Throughout the area. Almost
year round.

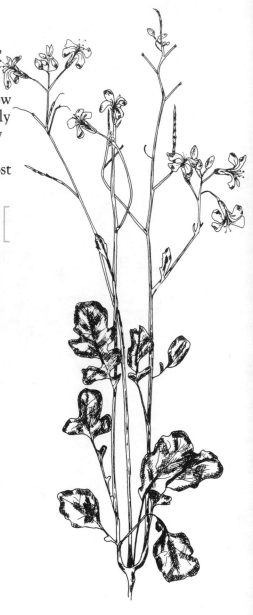

Maritime Ground-Cherry, Husk Tomato

Physalis viscosa ssp. *maritima* (M. A. Curtis) Waterfall
Nightshade

Perennial herb with deep-seated rhizome. Leaves alternate, entire (oval to oblong), both surfaces densely woolly. Flower yellow, bell-like, with 5 petals and dark center (see enlarged sketch); sepals form balloonlike husk or bladder with tomatolike fruit inside. May be eaten raw, used in stews, baked in dough as small pie. Sandy shores and dunes along coast. Kill Devil Hills. End of May through summer.

Common or Meadow Buttercup
Ranunculus acris L.
Crowfoot

Perennial herb, common,
native of Europe, erect, up to
3 feet tall. Leaves palmately
lobed, alternate. Flower yellow, 5 petaled. Considered a
medicinal herb with healing
properties for skin diseases.
Damp sand. Kill Devil Hills
near sound. April–May.

Dotted Horsemint

Monarda punctata L.
Mint

Perennial herb, 2 to 3 feet
tall. Stem simple to branched,
square. Leaves spicy, fragrant,
opposite. Flower petals yellow
spotted with purple; bracts at
base have a variety of white to
pink and lavender tints, seem-
ingly determined by sun expo-
sure, soil content, or plant
age. Sand dunes. Throughout
all the dune area. July–frost.

False Foxglove
Aureolaria flava (L.) Farw.
Figwort

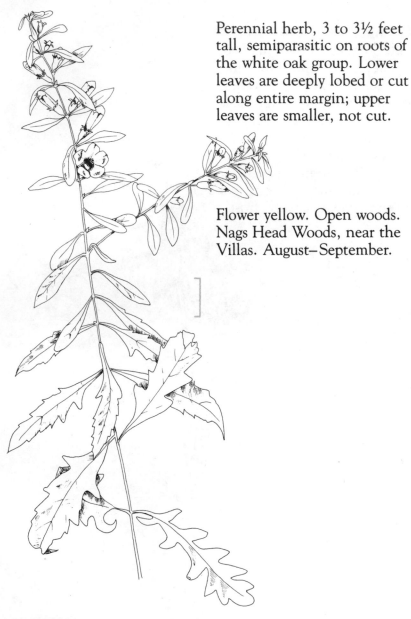

Perennial herb, 3 to 3½ feet tall, semiparasitic on roots of the white oak group. Lower leaves are deeply lobed or cut along entire margin; upper leaves are smaller, not cut.

Flower yellow. Open woods. Nags Head Woods, near the Villas. August–September.

Yellow or Carolina Jessamine
Gelsemium sempervirens (L.) Aiton f.
Logania

Perennial native, high climbing. Leaves opposite, waxy, dark, nearly evergreen. Flowers yellow and very fragrant, a colorful sight in early spring. All parts are POISONOUS to humans and livestock if eaten; deer are unaffected. Thickets, woodlands, roadsides. Near Route 158 bypass; throughout the area. February–March.

Common Evening Primrose
Oenothera biennis L.
Evening Primrose

Biennial herb, 1 to 6 feet tall,
most noticeable in May growing with marsh grasses. Stem
erect, somewhat hairy as are
the leaves. Flower yellow with
lemon fragrance, 1 to 2 inches
across, opens in late after-
noon. Near marshy areas.
Kitty Hawk Bay; Caffeys Inlet. May–end of October.

Beach Evening Primrose,
Seaside Evening Primrose
Oenothera humifusa Nuttall
Evening Primrose

Perennial herb, prostrate and
hoary. Flower yellow, turning
reddish, closes at midday and
opens again later. Dune hol-
lows, sandy sea beaches,
grows within 100 feet of ocean
surf. Throughout the area.
May–June.

Woolly Mullein
Verbascum thapsus L.
Figwort

Perennial or biennial herb,
native of Europe, 2 to 3 feet
tall. Stem and leaves yellow-
green and flannellike. Flowers
yellow, fragrant, on tall
spikes. Grown in early gardens for woolly absorbent
leaves which were believed to
have healing properties. Used
as "bandage" for wounds to
absorb blood; also smoked by
Indians to relieve asthma.
Roadsides, dry sand.
Throughout the area. Early
June–late autumn.

Section III

Orange or Maroon Flowers

Yellow Milkwort, Candy Weed
Polygala lutea L.
Milkwort

Biennial herb, sometimes a
short-lived perennial, 6 to 12
inches tall. Leaves succulent,
in a rosette at base of plant
and alternate upward. Flower
head compact; brilliant
orange. Wet roadsides,
ditches. Wanchese Road.
May–June.

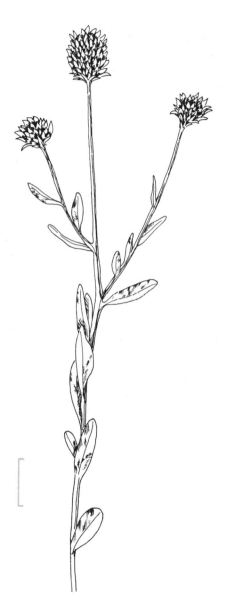

Marsh Milkweed
Asclepias lanceolata Walter
Milkweed

Perennial herb with milky
sap, about 4 feet tall. Stem
not branched, slender. Leaves
long, narrow, and opposite.
Flowers orange, lobes re-
flexed. Wet roadsides.
Wanchese Road. Mid-June–
August.

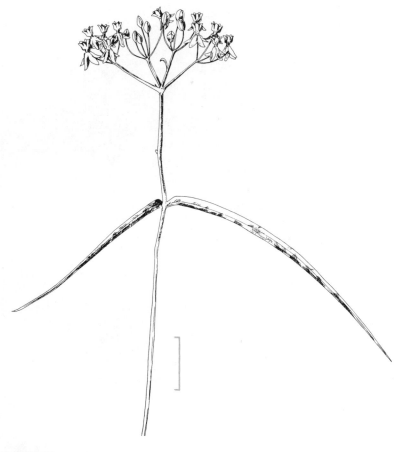

Butterfly-Weed, Pleurisy-Root
Asclepias tuberosa L.
Milkweed

Perennial herb, native, 8 inches to 2½ feet tall. Stem stout, erect, sap not milky. Leaves numerous, alternate, 2 to 3 inches long. Flower brilliant orange, long lasting and favored by butterflies. Medicinal properties known to Indians and early settlers.

This genus was named by Linnaeus for the Greek god of medicine, Asclepius, son of Apollo, called Aesculapius by the Romans. Dry, open woods. Road through Kitty Hawk Woods; Nags Head Woods. June–July.

Orange or Maroon Flowers 57

Coral or Trumpet Honeysuckle
Lonicera sempervirens L.
Honeysuckle

Perennial, woody, climbing or trailing vine. Leaves opposite, partially evergreen; leaves below flowers are united and surround the stem. Flowers long, tubular, red, yellow inside, but appear orange. Sunny thickets, edges of woods. Road along Kitty Hawk Bay; throughout the area. March–June.

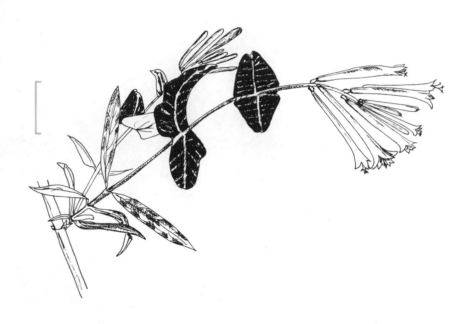

Trumpet Vine or Creeper, Cow-Itch

Campsis radicans (L.) Seemann

Bignonia

Vine, chiefly tropical, woody, trailing or climbing; long-lived if given full sun and protection from salty sea winds. Leaves opposite, pinnately divided. Flower a striking red-orange. Seed pod 10 to 12 inches long, forms in fall. Sunny roadsides. Duck Road; behind Jockey's Ridge; throughout the area. June–July and later.

Rattle Box
Daubentonia punicea (Cav.) DC.
Bean

Shrub, uncommon, 6 feet tall. Escaped from culti- vation, native to tropical America. Leaves alternate, pinnately compound with numerous leaflets. Flowers red-orange, pea shaped. Seed pod (see small sketch) forms in fall; a hard-coated 4 angled legume, 3 inches long, with seeds rattling inside. Seeds

POISONOUS to livestock, especially poultry and sheep. Sandy soil. Old Nags Head Cove; along Roanoke Sound; Wanchese Road; Hatteras Village. End of May–later.

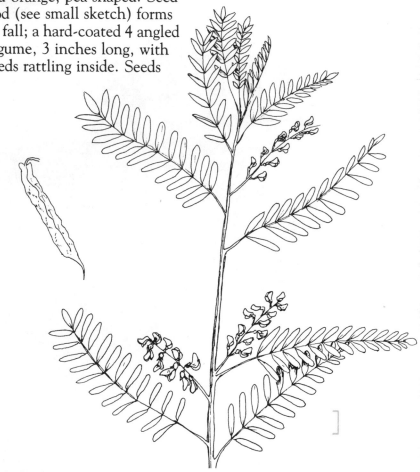

Gaillardia, Blanket Flower
Gaillardia pulchella Foug.
Aster

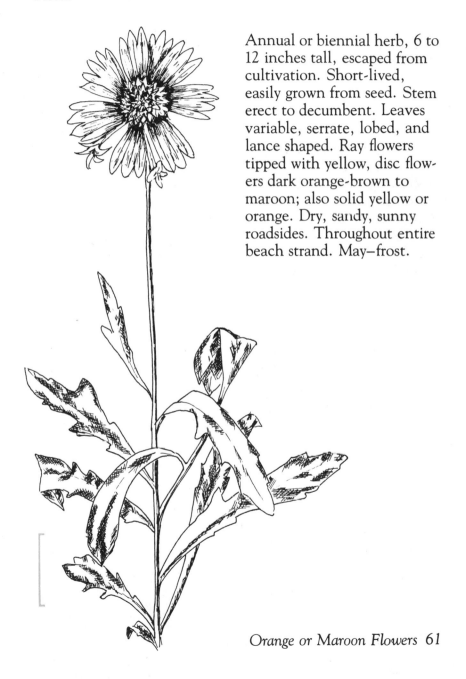

Annual or biennial herb, 6 to 12 inches tall, escaped from cultivation. Short-lived, easily grown from seed. Stem erect to decumbent. Leaves variable, serrate, lobed, and lance shaped. Ray flowers tipped with yellow, disc flowers dark orange-brown to maroon; also solid yellow or orange. Dry, sandy, sunny roadsides. Throughout entire beach strand. May–frost.

Groundnut, Indian Potato
Apios americana Medicus
Bean

Perennial twining vine. Leaves alternate, pinnately compound with 5 to 7 oval to lance-shaped leaflets. Flower fragrant, pea shaped, maroon or chocolate, elongated clusters. Tuberous root enlargements up to 2½ inches (see sketch) provide excellent wild food when fried, roasted or boiled in heavily salted water and served hot with butter. Seeds are also edible. "Openauk" is the Indian name. De-scribed by Thomas Hariot in 1588 as "a kind of roots of round form the size of a walnut, some far greater. Found in moist marshy ground growing many together one by another forming ropes, fastened like with a string." Believed to be the potato brought back to England from the New World. Along lagoons and wetlands. Throughout the area. July–September.

Section IV

Pink or Red Flowers

Moccasin Flower, Pink Lady's Slipper
Cyripedium acaule Aiton
Orchis

Erect herb, 6 to 15 inches tall.
Leaves 2 or more at base.
Flower pink, beautifully col-
ored. Picking is discouraged.
Dry pine groves, Woodland,
eastern border, Nags Head;
Roanoke Island. June.

Beach Morning Glory
Calystegia soldanella (L.) R. Brown
Morning Glory

Perennial prostrate vine with
alternate heart-shaped leaves.
Flowers pink to rose-purple,
funnel shaped. Rare, in North
Carolina grows only in Dare
County. Dry beach dunes.
Kitty Hawk Beach. April.

Arrowleaf Morning Glory
Ipomoea sagittata Cav.
Morning Glory

Perennial native, trailing or twining; primarily tropical. Leaves narrow, alternate. Flowers rose-lavender. Sap usually milky. Some related species are noxious weeds. Moist sandy roadsides, marshes. West section of Kitty Hawk. July–September.

Carolina Wild Pink
Silene caroliniana Walt.
Pink

Perennial native herb, barely 6 inches tall. Tuft of leaves at base; middle stem leaves opposite. Flowers pale to bright pink. Sandy open woods, edges of wooded paths and roads. Kitty Hawk Woods; Nags Head Woods; Southern Shores. April–May.

Annual Phlox
Phlox drummondii Hooker
Polemonium

Annual herb, erect, up to 12
inches tall; Texas native,
escaped from cultivation.
Upper leaves alternate, lower
(not shown) opposite. Flowers white to pink to red or
variegated. Sandy roadsides.
Kitty Hawk Village; Duck
Village; Nags Head. Late
April–June, sometimes later.

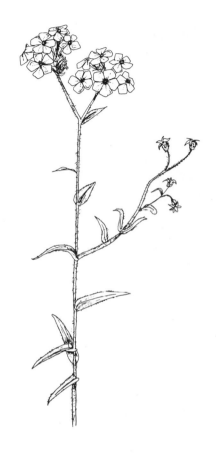

Salt-Marsh Fleabane, Camphorweed
Pluchea purpurascens (Schwartz) DC.
Aster

Annual or perennial herb,
1 to 3 feet tall, sticky, cam-
phor smelling; though growing in large colonies in Dare
County, it is limited to the
coastal plain. Heads of pink
rayless flowers in flattish terminal clusters, fragrant. Salt
marshes, brackish areas. Duck
Road north end. August–
October.

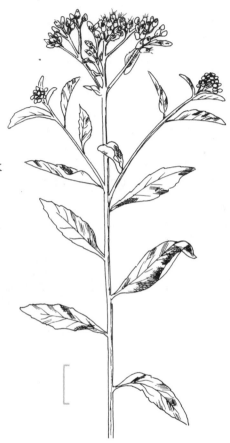

Swamp Milkweed

Asclepias incarnata ssp. *pulchra* (Willd.) Woodson
Milkweed

Perennial native herb, 2 to 3
feet tall. Stem has few
branches. Leaves opposite,
hairy beneath. Flowers pink,
lobes reflexed, numerous in
many-flowered terminals.
Seed pod elongated and
smooth (see sketch). Wet
roadsides, along sounds.
Southern Shores; Duck Road
north end. August–Sep-
tember.

Maryland Meadow-Beauty
Rhexia mariana L.
Meadow-Beauty

Perennial herb, 8 to 18 inches
tall. Stem square, quite hairy.
Leaves opposite. Flower pink
to purple; anthers large and
yellow. Brownish urn-shaped
seed pod; compared to a cream
pitcher by Thoreau. Wet
roadsides. Wanchese Road;
Kitty Hawk Village; Hatteras.
Usually August.

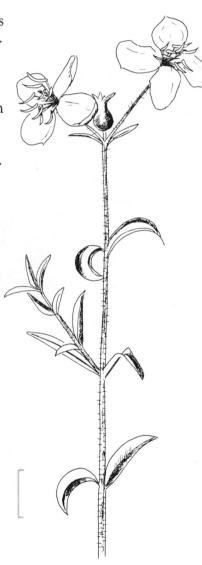

Large Marsh Pink, Sea-Pink
Sabatia dodecandra (L.) BSP.
Gentian

Perennial native herb, 1 to 2
feet tall. Leaves opposite.
Flower pink, showy, varying
from 9 to 12 petals. Painting
of another species, S. *gracilis*,
was labeled "Gentian" by
John White, governor and
artist of the Lost Colony;
Sabatia is unlike gentian, although in the same family.
Wet banks, sunny bays. Duck
Road north end; Roanoke
Island. August–October.

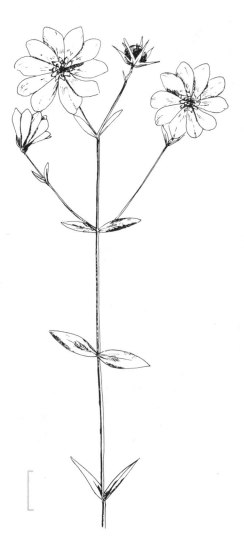

Climbing Hempweed, Boneset
Mikania scandens (L.) Willd.
Aster

Perennial twining vine.
Leaves opposite, varying from
oval to triangular. Flowers
dusty pink in small heads.
Marshes, wet areas, thickets.
Currituck Banks near Caffeys
Inlet; lagoons elsewhere.
July–October.

Daisy Fleabane, Common Fleabane
Erigeron philadelphicus L.
Aster

Short-lived perennial herb, 6 to 18 inches tall. Stem downy. Stem leaves clasping, basal leaves dandelionlike. Flower head ½ to 1 inch across, center yellow surrounded by 100 to 150 pink ray flowers. Wet roadsides. Kitty Hawk Bay; Southern Shores. April–June.

Showy Evening Primrose
Oenothera speciosa Nuttall
Evening Primrose

Perennial herb, up to 1½ feet tall, uncommon in Dare County. Leaves vary from plant to plant, both in length and size. Flowers showy pink to white. Wet road banks. Wanchese Harbor; Manteo streets. May.

Gerardia, False Foxglove
Agalinis purpurea (L.) Pennell
Figwort

Annual herb, profusely
branched, 1 to 4 feet tall,
semiparasitic on roots of
grasses and herbs. Flower deep
pink with purple-spotted yellow throat. Wet areas,
marshes. Nags Head to
Roanoke Island causeway.
August–frost.

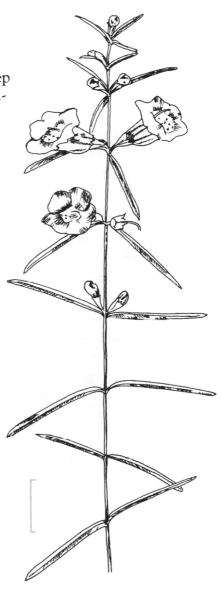

Swamp Rose
Rosa palustris Marshall
Rose

Perennial upright shrub, bushy up to 6 feet tall, rhizomatous. Leaves alternate, with 5 to 7 leaflets. Stipules narrow; thorns hooked, curved downward. Flowers pale pink; calyx bristly. Fruit is a red hip (see small sketch), rich in vitamin C, used for jam. Wet areas, salt marshes. Kitty Hawk Village; Duck Road north end; Wanchese Road; Bodie Island. May–July, sporadically to October.

Swamp Rose Mallow
Hibiscus moscheutos L.
Mallow

Perennial herb, robust, 5 to 7 feet tall. Flower pink, large, hollyhocklike. The first confection to be called "marshmallow" was derived from a sweet substance found in the roots of genus *Althaea officinalis*, also in the mallow family. The sticky sweet gum is also made into cough drops. In early times, mallow was used as a cure for sore throat and toothache, and made into an ointment for chilblains and chapped hands. Duck Road north end; Kitty Hawk Bay; continuing to Hatteras. August–September.

Dwarf Azalea
Rhododendron atlanticum (Ashe) Rehder
Heath

Perennial shrub, deciduous,
erect, up to 4 feet tall, forms
large colonies from numerous
rhizomes. Flowers pink, tubular. Seed pod shown in small
sketch. Uncommon in this
area. Margins of woods, damp
roadsides. Wanchese Road,
west side. Mid-April, August.

Trailing Wild Bean
Strophostyles helvola (L.) Ell.
Bean

Annual, trailing or twining vine, salt resistant. Leaves alternate. Flowers pink, turning yellowish with age. Seeds, germinating in spring, by midsummer can cover a dune with a green mat; dried seeds are a good food for birds. Beach, open woods, dunes. Duck Road to Hatteras. June–September.

Cardinal Flower
Lobelia cardinalis L.
Bluebell

Perennial native herb. Stem
2 feet tall. Leaves thin, numerous, alternate. Flower a
brilliant red; the shape of the
corolla resembles a cardinal's
miter, hence the name "of the
cardinal." Wet lagoon and
sound banks. Southern
Shores; Kitty Hawk. Late
summer.

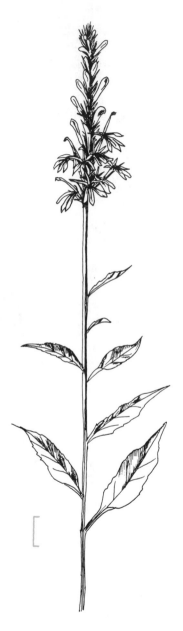

Section V

Blue or Purple Flowers

Blue-Eyed Grass

Sisyrinchium mucronatum var. *atlanticum* (Bicknell) Ahles
Iris

Native, stiff, grasslike winter annual, common, 4 to 16 inches tall. Flowers have six blue petals, each tipped with a small point; center of flowers yellow. A lovely sight in large fields. Sandy, moist roadsides and fields. Kitty Hawk Village; Bodie Island. Late April.

Dwarf or Vernal Iris
Iris verna L.
Iris

Perennial herb, 6 inches tall
when in bloom. Leaves narrow, straight, up to 12 inches
long when mature (unlike
crested iris). Fragrant blue-
violet flowers; sepals un-
crested, showing yellow or
orange band. If eaten in large
quantities, it is likely to cause
intestinal inflammation and
difficulty in breathing. Wet
ditches. Wanchese Road.
Early April.

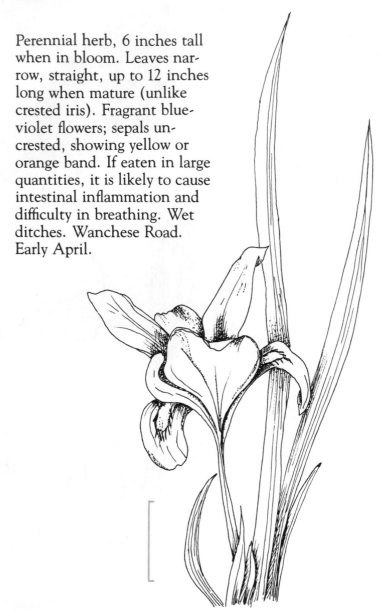

Slender Blue Flag
Iris prismatica Pursh ex Ker.
Iris

Perennial, 20 inches tall.
Leaves long, narrow, almost
grasslike. Flowers divided into
threes: 3 sepals bluish purple,
veined in white toward the
center; 3 erect petals lavender
to bluish violet. Slender rhizomes spread to form large
colonies. Uncommon in
North Carolina and considered rare in Dare County.
Marshes, wet ditches. Wanchese Road ditches. Mid-
May.

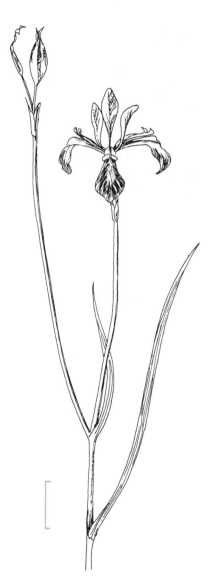

Blue or Old-Field Toadflax
Linaria canadensis (L.) Dumont
Figwort

Biennial native, 1 to 2 feet
tall. Stems erect, from basal
rosettes of prostrate leafy
stems. Leaves linear, shiny.
Pale violet flowers are two
lipped with a spur. Often covers fields in May. Sandy roadsides. Throughout the area.
Late April–mid-May.

Venus' Looking-glass
Specularia perfoliata (L.) A. DC.
Bluebell

Native annual herb, com-
mon, weedy, up to 1 foot tall.
Stems wandlike, encircled by
heart-shaped leaves. Flowers
tucked singly in the axils of
leaves, violet-blue with 5
spreading lobes. Open-
pollinated flowers ¼ to ½
inch. Smaller flowers are self-
pollinated and cleistogamous
(do not open). Dry, sandy
roadsides. Kitty Hawk traffic
island; Route 158 bypass;
throughout the area. April–
May.

Lyre-Leaved Sage
Salvia lyrata L.
Mint

Perennial native herb, 12 to 18 inches tall. Stems square, plant aromatic. Leaves lyre shaped, mostly basal, form a lasting rosette. Flowers blue-violet. Leaves of each of the more than 500 species of *Salvia* used as a cure for mouth infections and bleeding gums (*Salvia* derives from the Latin *salvere* meaning to heal). Sage used also for food flavoring, tea, mouthwash. Nags Head Woods; Roanoke Island roadsides. April–May.

Hyssop Skullcap
Scutellaria integrifolia L.
Mint

Native, slender, erect, leafy
perennial herb, 1 to 2 feet tall.
Leaves opposite, slender, not
toothed. Flowers strong blue,
two lipped, hooded. Also
known as narrow-leaved
skullcap. Wet, sunny roadsides and ditches. Wanchese
Road. Mid-June.

Mistflower, Ageratum
Eupatorium coelestinum L.
Aster

Perennial herb, 1 to 3 feet tall, forms colonies by long slender rhizomes. Stem solid, erect. Leaves opposite, arrow shaped. Flowers, in heads, form blue, fuzzy, flattopped clusters. Sunny moist areas. Kitty Hawk Village; roadsides and ditches. August–September.

Common Chicory, Blue Sailors
Cichorium intybus L.
Aster

Perennial herb, 1½ to 2 feet tall, infrequent in this area. Stem nearly naked. Basal leaves dandelionlike (small sketch not a basal leaf). Flowers in axils of upper leaves at ends of short branches; heads clear blue; rays square tipped, fringed, closed by noon. Used as medicine and eaten by ancient Romans; dried roots used in modern times to flavor coffee. Dry, sandy roadsides. Southern Shores Motor Lodge; roadside at Salvo. June–August.

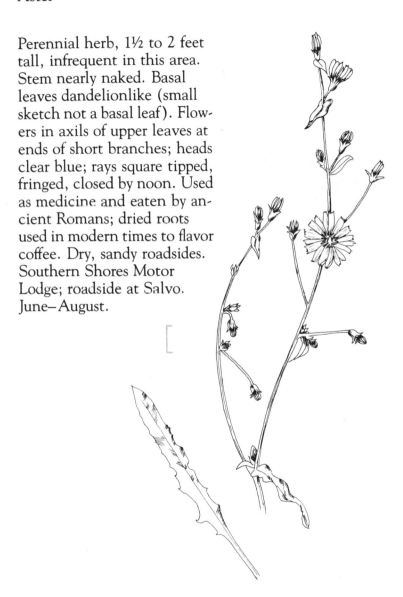

Longleaf Lobelia
Lobelia elongata Small
Bluebell

Perennial native herb, 1½ to
3 feet tall, rarely branched.
Leaves narrow, sharp
toothed, and alternate. Flowers deep blue with 2 narrow
lobes above, 3 narrow lobes
below. Marshes; Wild Swan
Lane, Southern Shores; Nags
Head. October.

Dayflower

Commelina communis L.

Spiderwort

Annual, erect or reclining weedy herb; numerous branches root at nodes and form large mats in growing season. Leaves alternate, clasping stem. Flowers with 2 blue petals and 1 whitish smaller petal appear singly every day or so from within the folds of greenish spathes. This is the only true blue flower in Eastern United States. Seeds provide food for songbirds, quail, mourning doves. Moist places, ditches, dry sandy dunes. Common throughout the area. Spring through summer.

Climbing Butterfly Pea

Centrosema virginianum (L.) Benth.

Bean

Perennial, trailing or climbing herb; most noticeable in August. Flower lavender, smaller than that of its cousin *Clitoria mariana* but more showy because of its profusion of blooms and climbing ability. Legume linear, flattened, about 4 inches long (see small sketch). Open sandy woods, clearings. Kitty Hawk; throughout the area. June, September.

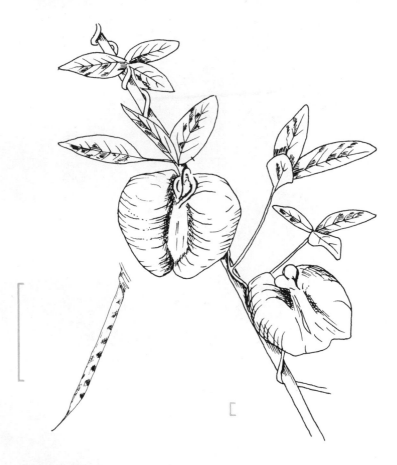

Maypops, Passion-Flower
Passiflora incarnata L.
Passion-Flower

Perennial woody vine, climbing or trailing, tendril bearing. Leaves deeply 3 lobed, alternate. Flower solitary, 5 petaled, purple, prominent elongated fringes at crown; styles 3, white, spreading. Fruit melon shaped, fleshy, greenish yellow, up to 2½ inches across, with many seeds fastened to outside wall; edible when ripe, "pop" if crushed. Often cultivated as an ornamental plant, although the network of stout running roots can soon become a nuisance. Thickets, woods, along fences. Throughout the area. May–October.

Pickerelweed
Pontederia cordata L.
Pickerelweed

Perennial native herb, stout,
1 to 4 feet tall, spreads in shallow water from thick, short
rhizomes. Leaves large, arrow
shaped. Flowers in erect, narrow, blue spike. Marshes,
roadside ditches. Duck Village north; Kitty Hawk Bay;
highway to Hatteras. June–
September.

Stalked Flower Aster
Aster racemosus Ellis
Aster

Perennial herb, infrequent in area, up to 40 inches tall. Stem stiffly erect, prominently angled, ash colored, densely powdered or dusty. Leaves narrow, lance shaped, with minute soft hairs. Flowers purple to lavender in heads on ascending branches. Along brackish lagoons and marshes. Southern Shores. October.

Sea Holly
Eryngium maritimum L.
Parsley

Perennial herb, introduced from northwestern European shores, 8 to 20 inches tall, erect or spreading, salt resistant. Stems numerous. Leaves gray-green, stiff, spiny, deeply lobed or incised. Flowers blue-lavender in compact ball-like head, subtended by spiny stiff bracts. In early times the aromatic roots were thought to be a cure for hopeless illnesses and injuries, melancholia, broken bones, and snake bite. It also produces a sugar that can be used in the preparation of sweetmeats. Very rare in southern-most limit; grows close to surf and within 50 feet of ocean. Transplanting is difficult because of its long carrotlike root. Propagated by seed and cuttings in late August. Hot sandy soil. Barrier dune near ocean. July–September.

Section VI

Green,
Inconspicuous,
or Without
Flowers

American Holly
Ilex opaca Aiton
Holly

Evergreen tree or shrublike
plant in coastal areas; separate
male and female plants. Bark
smooth gray. Leaves oblong,
leathery, prickly, dull green
above, yellowish below, alternate. Flowers small and
white, appearing in spring.
Fruit a red berry; choice food
for birds. Wood is ivory white,
in demand for piano keys,
ship models, inlays. In woods
with hardwood trees. Southern Shores; Nags Head
Woods. May, fall, and winter.

Yaupon
Ilex vomitoria Aiton
Holly

Shrub or small tree, 5 to 15
feet tall, admired by early
colonists; much like box-
wood, lends itself to trimming
and shaping into hedges, as in
the double row around the
Knot Garden in the Elizabethan Gardens on Roanoke
Island. Male and female
plants have numerous root
shoots. Bark has thin red-
brown scales. Leaves small,
evergreen, wavy-edged, oblong, leathery, alternate.
Drought and salt resistant.
Flowers small, greenish white.
Fruit, clear red, provides winter food for birds. Tea brewed
from dried leaves contains
caffeine. Maritime forests,
protected bay areas. Abun-
dant from Duck to Hatteras.
March–May, October–
November.

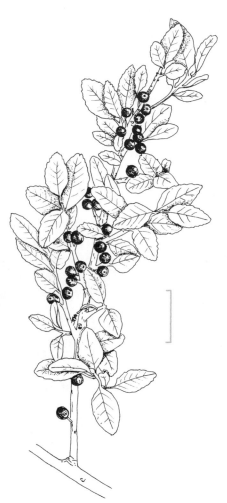

Dahoon, Cassena
Ilex cassine L.
Holly

Tree or shrub. Leaves shiny,
evergreen, smooth, alternate.
Flower white, small. Fruit, an
orange-red berry lasting
throughout the winter, is fine
food for birds. Sandy woods.
Buxton Woods is northern-
most area of growth. May–
June, October–November.

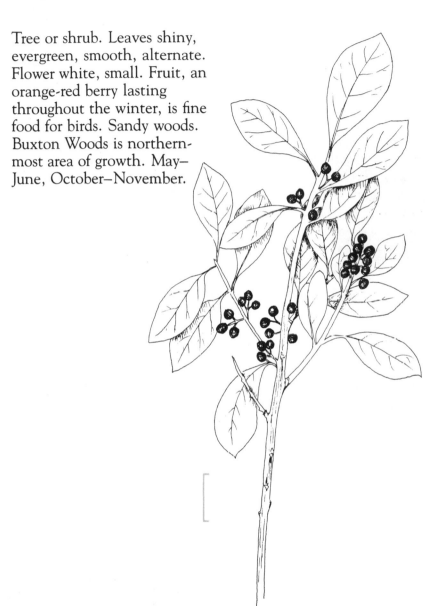

Red Cedar
Juniperus virginiana L.
Juniper

Native tree, medium size, pyramidal or spreading. Bark brown, shreddy; twisted into rope by Indians. Leaves are short scales: close overlapped pairs on older growth; longer and stiff pointed on young growth. Small cones form on male and female trees; mature female cone (see sketch) bluish, berrylike, appears in autumn. "Berries" are boiled to produce brown to khaki-colored dye and are used as flavoring in cooking; they furnish food for over 50 species of birds. Twigs are boiled for oxblood-brown dye, with addition of fixative, and with leaves are used as poultice for treatment of wounds. Wood strong, durable, is used for chests, cabinets, fence posts, and paneling in Outer Banks cottages. Heartwood grave markers are still visible in old cemeteries. It is damaged by salt spray and pruned by northeast winds near the oceanfront. Sunny, sandy soil. January, October–November.

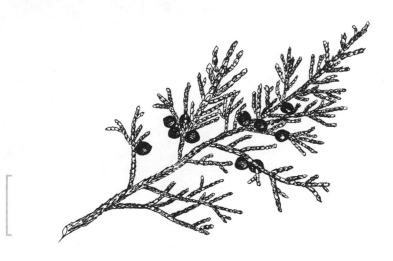

Loblolly Pine
Pinus taeda L.
Pine

Evergreen tree, 80 to 100 feet
tall, not salt resistant; crown
open with lower limbs drooping. Bark cinnamon colored.
Needles in bundles of 3, not
glossy, 5 to 10 inches long.
Male and female cones grow
on the same tree. Female cone
shown in sketch. This species
is distinctive for volume of
pollen shed by male cones in
spring. Wooded areas.
Throughout the area. March–
April, October.

Bald Cypress
Taxodium distichum (L.) Richard
Redwood

Deciduous tree, native of Southern swamps, grows to 140 feet tall; shape conical when young; crown irregular, flattopped when older. Bark rough, light gray to brownish red. Leaves are flat, light green needles. Male and female cones on the same tree; male cones in drooping clusters, shed pollen March–April; female cones large and round, shed seeds in October. The seeds furnish food for cranes and songbirds. Knees are sent up from wide spreading roots. Heartwood is used extensively in building boats, vats, pilings, caskets, or other objects requiring high decay resistance. Wet areas throughout.

Dwarf Palmetto
Sabal minor (Jacquin) Persoon
Palm

Low shrub, 2 to 4 feet tall, stem not erect. Leaves palmately divided as on a palm tree. Flowers creamy white but inconspicuous; fruited branch shown in sketch. A peripheral species in North Carolina. It is successfully grown in the moderate winter climate of Hatteras, but suffers cold injury in the northern extension of that range. Sandy soil. Buxton-Hatteras area. May–July, September–November.

Spanish Moss
Tillandsia usneoides L.
Pineapple

Native tropical plant, grows
in trees only in coastal plain;
pendant gray, rootless
epiphyte, not a parasite or
true moss; falls in striking
cascades. Flower inconspicuous, yellowish green. Fruit
shown enlarged. Once used as
mattress stuffing and for dia-
pers by local Indians (John
Lawson, 1709). Patches
throughout in moist wooded
areas. April–June.

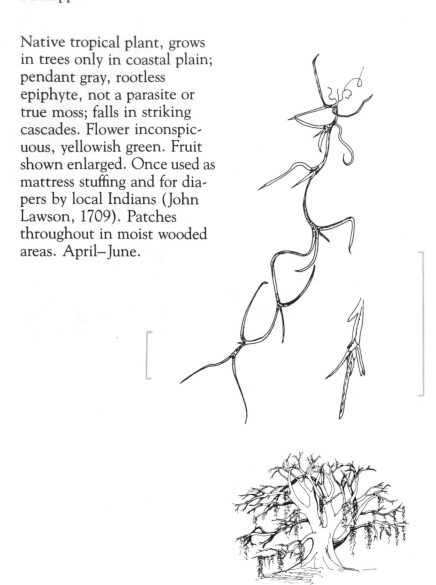

Mistletoe
Phoradendron serotinum (Raf.) M. C. Johnston
Mistletoe

Tropical native parasite, woody, yellowish green. Stem jointed and many branched. Leaves broad, opposite, evergreen. Flowers green. Berries white. This traditional Christmas decoration was regarded as sacred by ancient Gauls. POISONOUS if eaten. Grows in branches and trunks of deciduous trees. Throughout the area in woods. November–January, through spring.

Witch-Hazel
Hamamelis virginiana L.
Witch-Hazel

Shrub or small tree, deciduous. Leaf uneven, wavy toothed. Flower with 4 long, slender, yellow petals appears after leaves drop. Fruit is a woody capsule; at maturity it splits open, ejecting the seeds for great distances. Seeds provide food for animals and birds. Bark extract is used medicinally; branches are used as "divining rods" for the detection of underground water. Dry wooded areas. Nags Head Woods. September–December, fruit the following August.

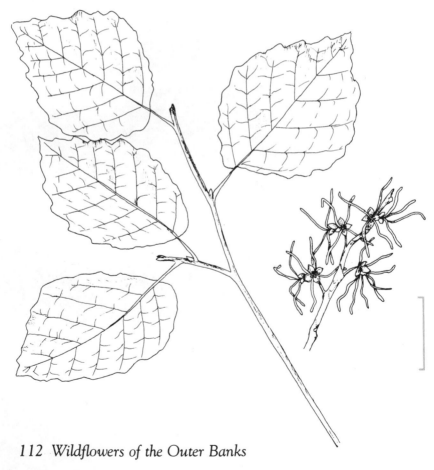

Persimmon
Diospyros virginiana L.
Ebony

Deciduous tree, up to 50 feet tall. Bark thick, dark, broken into squarish blocks. Leaves simple, alternate, oval. Flower (see small sketch) inconspicuous, yellowish, develops on twig of previous year. Fruit hard, astringent when green; pulpy sweet and edible when ripe in late fall. Wood heavy, hard, tough, dark brown to black; used for shoe lasts, shuttles, spools. Dry, open roadsides, dunes. May–June, September–October.

Live Oak
Quercus virginiana Miller
Beech

Evergreen tree with medium sensitivity to salt spray, grows large if protected from ocean by distance, dunes, or vegetative cover; shape and height are molded by wind or salt spray. Trunk short, bark furrowed dark brown; branches widespread, angular, pale gray. Leaf leathery, oblong to oval; dark green above, grayish hairy beneath; leaf lacks bristletip. Female flowers, inconspicuous; male flowers, drooping clusters of catkins. Wood very hard, strong and durable. Acorn was a staple food for early local Indians; bark is crushed for medicinal use. Several large, ancient specimens grow in the cemeteries of Kitty Hawk. Kitty Hawk; Nags Head Woods; Hatteras. April, September–November.

Sweet-Gum
Liquidambar styraciflua L.
Witch-Hazel

Deciduous tree, symmetrical, conical or flattopped, 50 to 140 feet tall. Bark regularly grooved, grayish. Leaves alternate, 3 to 5 lobed, toothed, hairless; flowers inconspicuous in spherical heads. Fruit cluster (shown in sketch) a dry, prickly, long-stemmed hanging ball; seeds are fine food for birds and squirrels. Name alludes to sap that oozes from cuts in the bark. Wood is used for furniture veneer, lumber, plywood. Nags Head Woods; throughout area in woods. April–May, September–November.

Swamp Willow
Salix caroliniana (Michaux) Petrides
Willow

Southern native tree, wind pruned here but up to 35 feet tall elsewhere. Bark gray, scaly to furrowed; twigs reddish, hairy, or somewhat hairy beneath. Leaves deciduous, alternate, long narrow pointed, whitish on underside. Male and female flowers on separate trees; male most conspicuous, fluffy, attracts butterflies and bees; female (see sketch) pale yellow, forms catkins. Twigs are used for basket weaving. Moist areas. Duck Road; Nags Head Woods. March–April.

Hercules'-Club, Prickly Ash, Toothache Tree
Zanthoxylum clava-herculis L.
Rue

Native deciduous tree, up to 20 feet tall, moderately salt resistant. Bark thin, smooth, gray, with scattered corky knobs. Thorns stout, ½ inch long, scattered over surface of twigs. Leaves alternate, lemon fragrant when crushed; leaflets hairless, shiny, curved. Flowers small, white, in large terminal cluster. Fruit (see sketch) in late summer. Bark has been chewed since early times as a toothache remedy; ripe berries were mixed with hot water by Indians and early colonists for mouthwash. A sand binder, significant to local ecology. Sand dunes, maritime forests. Dry dunes, 200 feet or more from ocean. April–May, July–September.

Southern Wax Myrtle
Myrica cerifera L.
Wax Myrtle

Evergreen shrub, male and female plants, 10 to 30 feet tall, thrives in full sun and poor soil. Leaves alternate, wedge shaped, leathery, aromatic, and gold dotted below. Flowers inconspicuous, in early spring. Fruit small gray-white wax-covered berry on female plants in late summer. Wax is used for scented candles. Low sandy roadsides, along fresh ponds. Duck Village; throughout Outer Banks. April–June, August–October.

Eastern Hop Hornbeam
Ostrya virginiana (Miller) K. Koch
Hazel

Small deciduous tree, 20 to
30 feet tall, grows rarely in
coastal plain. Bark brown,
peeling, shreddy. Leaves yel-
low-green, oval, thin, tough,
hairy beneath. Male and female catkins on same tree.
Fruit cluster (shown in
sketch) of papery, bladderlike
sacs, each enclosing a nut.
Wood tough, cross-grained,
used for mallets, tool handles,
levers, fence posts. Rich low
woods. Juniper Trail, Southern Shores; Nags Head
Woods. April, September.

Summer or Pigeon Grape
Vitis aestivalis Michaux
Vine

High climbing, aggressive vine, one of 3 species of wild grapes still growing on Outer Banks. Leaf lobes shallow or deep. Flowers greenish. Fruit was considered marketable by John White, governor of the Lost Colony. The plant is use- ful as a sand binder. Fruit, an ingredient for excellent jelly, is also popular with birds. Hot, sunny, dry dunes. Jockey's Ridge State Park; Kill Devil Hills; Duck Road north end. May, September– October.

Seaside Pennywort, Large Leaf Pennywort
Hydrocotyle bonariensis Lam.
Parsley

Perennial ground creeper about 6 inches tall, salt resistant. Leaves shiny, bright green, almost round, slightly scalloped along edges. Flowers small, pale greenish white in umbels. Useful for landscaping and dune erosion control.

Moist sandy areas, also hot dry sand. Jockey's Ridge State Park on sound side; Southern Shores dunes; highway edges from Bodie Island to Hatteras. April–September.

Marsh Elder, Seaside Elder
Iva imbricata Walter
Aster

Native shrub, erect, 1 to 3½
feet tall, branched at base.
Leaves alternate, thickish.
Flower (see enlarged sketch)
small, greenish white, nodding. Salt resistant and useful
in dune erosion control. Hot
dry sand. Southern Shores
near ocean. August–October.

Glasswort, Chickenclaw Saltwort
Salicornia europaea L.
Goosefoot

Annual succulent, edible
salad-type green, about 8
inches tall; turns deep pink or
red in autumn. Stem jointed,
stiffly ascending, branching.
Flowers minute, green, sunk
into joints. Brackish marshes.
Near Bodie Island lighthouse;
under Oregon Inlet bridge.
July–October.

Common or Broad-Leaved Cat-Tail
Typha latifolia L.
Cat-Tail

Perennial aquatic, 4 to 8 feet tall, in large colonies. Leaves numerous, flat, swordlike. Spikes 3 to 12 inches long and 1 or more inches thick; lower spike bears brown female flowers; upper spike or tail bears paler male flowers and disappears later. Tender green spikes are edible if boiled a few minutes in salted water, doused with butter, and eaten hot. Shallow sound waters, ponds, ditches. Along all sounds. May–July.

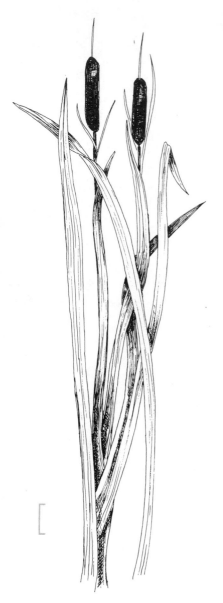

Florida Adder's Mouth
Malaxis spicata Swartz
Orchis

Perennial, usually 3 to 18
inches tall; rare in Dare
County, its northernmost
limit. Has 2 bright green
leaves. Flowers green, heart-
shaped lip pale yellow to
orange-vermillion. Moist
woods. Buxton Woods.
August–frost.

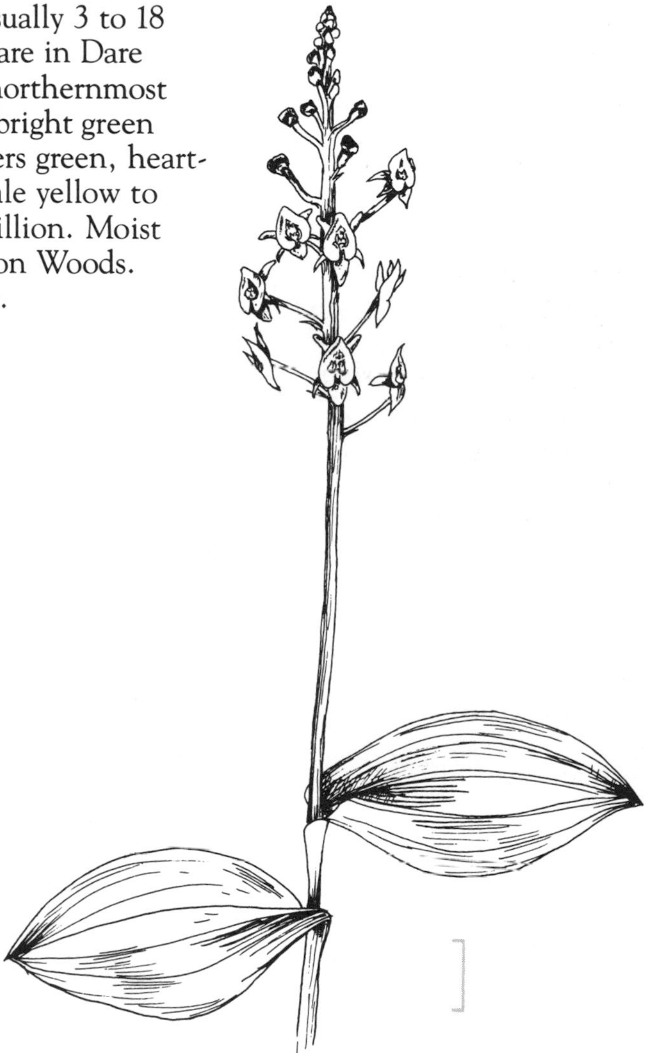

Ebony Spleenwort
Asplenium platyneuron (L.) Oakes
Spleenwort

Delicate fern with creeping
rhizome. Leafstalk and axis
lustrous, red-brown, brittle.
Leaves pinnately divided, 4 to
20 inches long, clustered,
deciduous. Sterile leaves are
pale green, shorter, spreading;
fertile leaves are more erect
with spores along the midrib
of leaflet. Cool dry woods.
Nags Head Woods; through-
out the area in woods. April–
October.

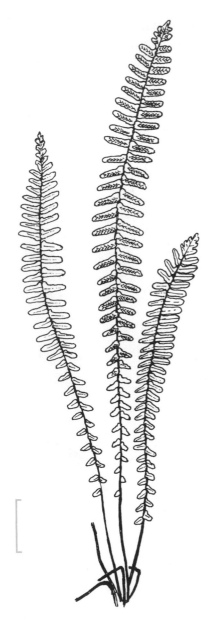

Virginia Chain-Fern
Woodwardia virginica (L.) Smith
Chain-Fern

Fern rhizome long, creeping, horizontal branching, dark and covered with brown lance-shaped scales. Leaf stalks are as long as blades. Leaves erect 1 to 2½ feet long; sterile and fertile leaves are similar. Spores (see small sketch) are in lines along the scaly midribs of leaflets. Acid soil, marshy wooded areas. In woods throughout the area. June–September.

Bracken Fern
Pteridium aquilinum (L.) Kuhn
Fern

Native fern, common, coarse; grows in poor soil, sun or shade, on deep and sunken rhizomes; forms large colonies. Leaf stalk is reddish toward base and yellowish above. Leaves erect, stiff, vary in length but average 18 inches; spores on margins of leaflets. It was used medicinally by ancients for internal disorders; the starchy root stocks furnished food for the Indians; new tops, when cooked like asparagus, may be eaten in moderation. Simmered for 20 minutes, young bracken tops produce a light green dye; rhizomes boiled for 2 hours will produce a yellow dye if chrome is added as a fixative; both suitable for dying wool. The plant is widespread in temperate parts of the Old World also. Patches throughout the area. July–September.

Royal Fern

Osmunda regalis var. *spectabilis* (Willd.) Gray

Royal Fern

Large coarse fern, up to 5 feet tall. Rhizomes are stout, woody, without scales, in massive clumps of old roots. Leaves in 2 forms, erect in dense crown; spores in brown terminal clusters. Early spring shoots, "fiddle heads," edible if cooked like asparagus. Marshes, moist wooded areas, March–June.

Sea Oats
Uniola paniculata L.
Grass

Perennial native grass, 3 or
more feet tall. Leaves are pale
green. Flower spikelets form
in late June. Propagation by
rhizomes is more certain than
by seeds. Has proven to be a
necessary sand binder on the
frontal dunes, very resistant to
wind and salt spray. Picking,
damaging, or destroying
plants is discouraged. From
sandy frontal dunes to woods
line. Throughout the area.
June–July, November.

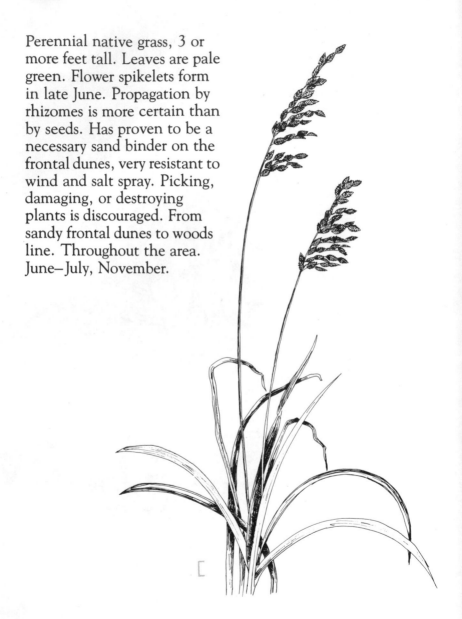

American Beach Grass
Ammophila breviligulata Fernald
Grass

Perennial, 1 to 3 feet tall, considered rare in North Carolina. Leaves tough, remain partly green in winter. Flower spike and stem are about 8 inches long. Plant spreads readily by underground rhizomes. It is an excellent sand binder and extremely salt resistant; most specimens seen on the frontal dunes have been planted. Frontal dunes throughout the area. August–September.

Saltmeadow Cordgrass
Spartina patens (Ait.) Muhl.
Grass

Perennial marsh grass, 1 to 5
feet tall, with an uncombed
tousled appearance. Rhizomes
underground; new growth
springs from flat mats of old
grass stems. Flat leaves readily
distinguish the grass family
from the rushes and sedges.
Flowers are inconspicuous.
Seeds are good food for migratory birds. Brackish marshes,
low dunes. Along sounds.
June–September.

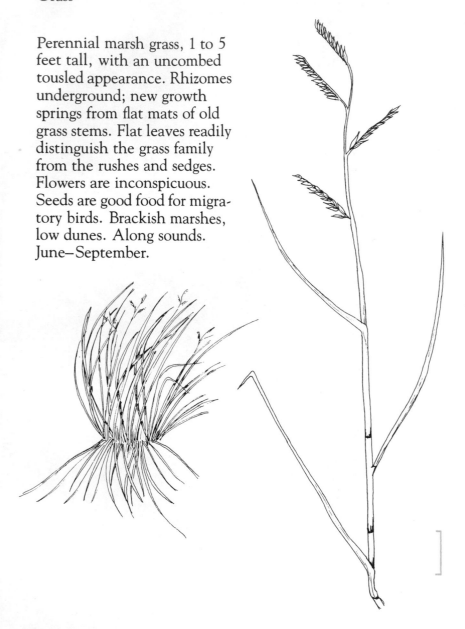

Needle Rush, Black Rush
Juncus roemerianus Scheele
Rush

Coarse, rigid plant, dense
stands appear blackish when
seen in certain lights. Leaves
needlelike, form clasping
sheaths open partway down
from tip. Flowers brownish in
branched clusters; used for
green dye. Brackish marshes.
Along sounds. May–October.

Whitetop Sedge
Dichromena colorata (L.) Hitchcock
Sedge

Plant grows up to 1 foot tall.
Triangular stem. Leaves are
long and very narrow except
at base. Flowers are minute, in
small spikes clustered at stem
top; 4 to 7 white bracts at top
are frequently mistaken for
the flower. Wet ditches, lagoons. Road from Nags Head
to Hatteras. May–September.

Cape Hatteras
National Seashore
Herbarium List

References

Rare and
Endangered
Species

Glossary

Index

3. *Lycopodiaceae* Clubmoss Family
Lycopodium appressum – southern bog clubmoss

7. *Osmundaceae* Royal Fern Family
Osmunda regalis var. *spectabilis* – royal fern

10. *Pteridaceae* Fern Family
Pteridium aquilinum – bracken

11. *Aspidiaceae* Shield Fern Family
Onoclea sensibilis – sensitive fern
Thelypteris palustris – marsh fern

12. *Blechnaceae* Chain-Fern Family
Woodwardia areolata – netted chain-fern
Woodwardia virginica – Virginia chain-fern

13. *Aspleniaceae* Spleenwort Family
Asplenium platyneuron – ebony spleenwort

14. *Polypodiaceae* Fern Family
Polypodium polypodioides – resurrection fern

15. *Azollaceae* Mosquito Fern Family
Azolla caroliniana – mosquito fern[n]

16. *Pinaceae* Pine Family
Pinus palustris – long-leaf pine
Pinus taeda – loblolly pine

17. *Taxodiaceae* Redwood Family
Taxodium distichum – bald cypress

18. *Cupressaceae* Juniper Family
Juniperus virginiana – red cedar

19. *Typhaceae* Cat-Tail Family
Typha augustifolia – narrow-leaved cat-tail
Typha domingensis – cat-tail
Typha glauca – glaucous cat-tail
Typha latifolia – common or broad-leaved cat-tail

24. *Zannichelliaceae*
Zannichellia palustris – horned pondweed

n. Newly recorded in Dare County.
s. New state record.

26. *Juncaginaceae* Arrow-Grass Family
   Triglochin striata – arrow grass
27. *Alismataceae* Water-Plantain Family
   Sagittaria falcata – arrowhead, duck potato
   Sagittaria graminea – grass leaved arrowhead
   Sagittaria latifolia var. *latifolia* – duck potato
   Sagittaria subulata var. *subulata* – arrowhead, duck potato
28. *Hydrocharitaceae* Frog's Bit Family
   Vallisneria americana – tapegrass, eelgrass
29. *Poacea* Grass Family
   Ammophila breviligulata – American beach grass
   Andropogon elliottii – beard grass
   Andropogon gerardii – turkeyfoot
   Andropogon scoparius – little bluestem
   Andropogon ternarius – beard grass
   Andropogon virginicus – broom-sedge
   Briza minor – quaking grass
   Cenchrus longispinus – sandspur
   Cenchrus tribuloides – sandspur
   Chloris petraea – finger grass
   Distichlis spicata – salt grass
   Echinochloa walteri – barnyard grass
   Eleusine indica – goosegrass
   Elymus virginicus – wild rye grass
   Eragrostis refracta – love grass
   Eragrostis spectabilis – purple love grass
   Erianthus alopecuroides – beardgrass, plumegrass
   Erianthus giganteus – plumegrass, sugar cane plumeweed
   Festuca elatior – fescue
   Festuca rubra – red fescue
   Leptochloa fascicularis – gray sprangletop
   Lolium perenne – rye grass
   Melica mutica – melic grass
   Mehlenbergia capillaris – purple muhly, hairgrass
   Panicum aciculare
   Panicum amarulum – silver bunchgrass
   Panicum amarum – running beach grass
   Panicum anceps var. *rhizomatum*
   Panicum commonsianum
   Panicum lanuginosum
   Panicum polyanthes
   Paspalum distichum – knot grass
   Paspalum laeve

Paspalum setaceum – paspalum
Phragmites communis – reed
Polypogon monspeliensis – rabbit's foot grass
Setaria geniculata – bristle grass, foxtail grass
Setaria magna – big foxtail, giant bristle grass
Sorghum halepense – Johnson grass
Spartina alterniflora – cordgrass, smooth cordgrass
Spartina cynosuroides – big cordgrass
Spartina patens – saltmeadow cordgrass
Sporobolus poiretii – smut-grass
Tridens flavus var. *flavus* – purple top
Triplasis purpurea – sand grass, purple sand grass
Uniola laxa
Uniola paniculata – sea oats
Zizania aquatica – wild rice

30. *Cyperaceae* Sedge Family
Carex alata – sedge
Carex albolutescens
Carex glaucescens
Carex kobomugi
Carex sp.
Cladium jamaicense – saw-grass
Cyperus dipsaciformis
Cyperus filicinus – cyperus, sweet rush
Cyperus globulosus
Cyperus grayi
Cyperus odoratus
Cyperus polystachyos var. *texensis*
Cyperus retrorsus
Cyperus rotundus
Cyperus strigosus – sweet rush
Dichromena colorata – whitetop sedge
Eleocharis acicularis – spike rush
Eleocharis albida – spike rush
Eleocharis ssp.
Eleocharis tenuis
Fimbristylis spadicea – sand rush
Scirpus americanus – chair-maker's rush
Scirpus cyperinus – bulrush
Scirpus robustus – triangle sedge

31. *Arecaceae* Palm Family
Sabal minor – dwarf palmetto

32. *Araceae* Arum Family
    Peltandra virginica—arum

35. *Xyridaceae* Yellow-Eyed Grass Family
    Xyris torta—yellow-eyed grass

37. *Bromeliaceae* Pineapple Family
    Tillandsia usneoides—spanish moss

38. *Commelinaceae* Spiderwort Family
    Commelina communis—dayflower
    Commelina erecta—dayflower, dewflower
    Commelina virginica—dayflower[n]
    Tradescantia ohiensis—spiderwort[n]

39. *Pontederiaceae* Pickerelweed Family
    Pontederia cordata—pickerelweed

40. *Juncaceae* Rush Family
    Juncus acuminatus
    Juncus biflorus—rush
    Juncus bufonius—toad rush
    Juncus megacephalus—bur grass
    Juncus roemerianus—needle rush, black rush
    Juncus scirpoides—rush

41. *Liliaceae* Lily Family
    Allium bivalve—false garlic
    Allium canadense—wild onion
    Allium canadense var. *canadense*—wild onion
    Hemerocallis fulva—tawny day-lily
    Polygonatum biflorum—Solomon's seal
    Smilax auriculata—greenbrier
    Smilax bona-nox—greenbrier, catbrier
    Smilax glauca—wild bamboo
    Smilax rotundifolia—catbrier
    Yucca filamentosa—spoonleaf yucca, beargrass

44. *Amaryllidaceae* Amaryllis Family
    Hypoxis micrantha—yellow star grass

46. *Iridaceae* Iris Family
    Iris prismatica—slender blue flag
    Iris verna—dwarf or vernal iris
    Iris virginica—blue iris[n]
    Sisyrinchium arenicola—blue-eyed grass
    Sisyrinchium mucronatum var. *atlanticum*—blue-eyed grass
    Sisyrinchium rosulatum—blue-eyed grass

49. *Orchidaceae* Orchis Family
   Calopogon pulchellus – grass pink
   Cypripedium acaule – moccasin flower, pink lady's slipper
   Goodyera pubescens – downy rattle-snake plantain[n]
   Habenaria blephariglottis – white fringed-orchid
   Habenaria ciliaris – yellow fringed-orchid
   Listera australis – southern twayblade[n]
   Malaxis spicata – Florida adder's mouth
   Malaxis unifolia – green adder's mouth[n]
   Pogonia ophioglossoides – rose pogonia[n]
   Spiranthes cernua var. *odorata* – autumn ladies' tresses[n]
   Spiranthes gracilis – slender ladies' tresses[n]
   Spiranthes praecox – ladies' tresses, grass-leaved ladies' tresses
   Spiranthes vernalis – spring ladies' tresses
   Tipularia discolor – crane fly-orchid[n]

50. *Saururaceae* Lizard's Tail Family
   Saururus cernuus – lizard's tail[n]

51. *Salicaceae* Willow Family
   Populus alba – silver poplar, white poplar
   Populus deltoides – common cottonwood
   Salix babylonica – weeping willow
   Salix caroliniana – swamp willow

52. *Myricaceae* Wax-Myrtle Family
   Myrica cerifera – southern wax myrtle
   Myrica pennsylvanica – bayberry, candleberry

53. *Juglandaceae* Walnut Family
   Carya cordiformis – bitternut hickory[n]
   Juglans nigra – black walnut

54. *Betulaceae* Hazel Family
   Carpinus caroliniana – ironwood, American hornbeam
   Ostrya virginiana – eastern hop hornbeam

55. *Fagaceae* Beech Family
   Castanea pumila – chestnut, chinquapin
   Fagus grandifolia – American beech
   Quercus falcata – Spanish oak, southern red oak
   Quercus incana – blue-jack oak, upland willow oak
   Quercus laurifolia – laurel oak
   Quercus marilandica – blackjack oak
   Quercus nigra – water oak
   Quercus stellata – post oak
   Quercus virginiana – live oak

57. *Moraceae* Mulberry Family
Broussonetia papyrifera – paper mulberry[n]
Ficus carica – fig, common fig

59. *Urticaceae* Nettle Family
Boehmeria cylindrica – bog hemp, false nettle
Boehmeria cylindrica var. *drummondiana*

61. *Loranthaceae* Mistletoe Family
Phoradendron serotinum – mistletoe

63. *Polygonaceae* Buckwheat Family
Polygonum glaucum – seabeach knotweed, knotweed
Polygonum hydropiper – marshpepper smartweed
Polygonum hydropiperoides – smartweed
Polygonum hydropiperoides var. *opelousanum*
Polygonum pensylvanicum – Pennsylvania smartweed
Polygonum punctatum – water smartweed
Rumex acetosella – sheep-sorrel, sourgrass[n]
Rumex crispus – yellow dock
Rumex hastatulus – sorrel, dock, sheep-sorrel
Rumex pulcher – seabeach dock[n]

64. *Chenopodiaceae* Goosefoot Family
Atriplex arenaria – seabeach orach
Salicornia bigelovii – glasswort, dwarf saltwort
Salicornia europaea – glasswort, chickenclaw saltwort
Salicornia virginica – perennial saltwort

66. *Amaranthaceae* Amaranth Family
Alternanthera philoxeroides – alligator weed[n]
Amaranthus cannabinus – water-hemp
Amaranthus hybridus – green amaranth, pigweed[n]
Amaranthus pumilis

68. *Phytolaccaceae* Pokeweed Family
Phytolacca americana – pokeweed

69. *Aizoaceae* Carpetweed Family
Sesuvium maritimum – sea-purslane

71. *Caryophyllaceae* Pink Family
Cerastium glomeratum – mouse-ear chickweed
Cerastium holosteoides var. *vulgare*
Paronychia riparia
Saponaria officinalis – soapwort, bouncing bet[n]
Scleranthus annuus – knawl[n]
Silene caroliniana – Carolina wild pink

Spergularia marina—sandy spurrey
Stellaria media—common chickweed

76. *Ranunculaceae* Crowfoot Family
    Clematis virginiana—virgin's bower[n]
    Ranunculus acris—common or meadow buttercup[n]
    Ranunculus bulbosus—bulbous buttercup[n]
    Ranunculus sceleratus—buttercup

80. *Magnoliaceae* Magnolia Family
    Liriodendron tulipifera—tulip tree
    Magnolia virginiana—sweet bay, white bay

81. *Annonaceae* Custard-Apple Family
    Asimina parviflora—dwarf pawpaw

84. *Lauraceae* Laurel Family
    Persea borbonia—red bay
    Sassafras albidum—sassafras
    Sassafras albidum var. *molle*—sassafras

86. *Fumariaceae* Fumitory Family
    Corydalis micrantha ssp. *australis*—slender or yellow fumewort[n]

88. *Brassicaceae* Mustard Family
    Arabidopsis thaliana—mouse-ear cress
    Cakile edentula—sea rocket
    Cardamine hirsuta—bitter cress
    Coronopus didymus
    Lepidium virginicum—poor-man's pepper
    Raphanus raphanistrum—wild radish[n]
    Sibara virginica

89. *Sarraceniaceae* Pitcher-Plant Family
    Sarracenia flava—trumpets, biscuit flowers

94. *Saxifragaceae* Saxifrage Family
    Decumaria barbara—climbing hydrangea

95. *Hamamelidaceae* Witch-Hazel Family
    Hamamelis virginiana—witch-hazel[n]
    Liquidambar styraciflua—sweet gum

97. *Rosaceae* Rose Family
    Amelanchier arborea—serviceberry
    Amelanchier canadensis—juneberry, serviceberry, shadbush
    Amelanchier obovalis—juneberry, serviceberry
    Potentilla canadensis—common cinquefoil, five fingers[n]
    Potentilla recta—rough-fruited cinquefoil[n]
    Prunus augustifolia—chicksaw plum[n]

Prunus serotina – black cherry
Rosa palustris – swamp rose
Rosa wichuraiana – memorial rose, Dorothy Perkins rose
Rubus argutus – highbush blackberry
Rubus trivialis – southern dewberry
Sorbus arbutifolia – red chokeberry
Sorbus arbutifolia var. *atropurpurea* – purple chokeberry

98. *Fabaceae* Bean Family
Aeschynomene indica
Albizia julibrissin – mimosa, silk-tree
Amorpha fruticosa – lead plant, indigo bush
Apios americana – groundnut, Indian potato
Cassia fasciculata – partridge pea
Cassia nictitans – wild sensitive plant
Centrosema virginianum – climbing butterfly pea
Clitoria mariana – butterfly pea
Crotalaria angulata – rabbit-bells, rattle box
Daubentonia punicea – rattle box
Desmodium nudiflorum – beggar lice
Desmodium paniculatum – panicled tick-trefoil[n]
Desmodium strictum – beggar's-ticks
Galactia regularis – milk pea[n]
Lathyrus maritimus – beach pea[ns]
Lespedeza cuneata – sericea
Lespedeza virginica[n]
Lotus corniculatus – birdsfoot trefoil[n]
Lotus helleri – birdsfoot trefoil, bastard indigo[n]
Melilotus alba – white sweet clover
Melilotus officinalis – yellow sweet clover
Rhynchosia difformis – trailing rhynchosia
Robinia hispida – bristly locust[n]
Robinia pseudo-acacia – black locust
Strophostyles helvola – trailing wild bean
Strophostyles umbellata – pink sand bean
Trifolium arvense – rabbitfoot-clover
Trifolium campestre – low hop clover[n]
Trifolium dubium – low hop clover
Trifolium repens – white clover, west dutch clover
Vicia angustifolia – vetch
Vicia hugeri – wood vetch[ns]

99. *Linaceae* Flax Family
Linum virginianum – slender yellow flax[n]
Linum virginianum var. *floridanum* – slender yellow flax[n]
Linum virginianum var. *medium* – flax

100. *Oxalidaceae* Wood Sorrel Family
   Oxalis rubra – wood sorrel
   Oxalis violacea – violet wood sorrel[n]

101. *Geraniaceae* Geranium Family
   Geranium carolinianum – wild geranium, cranesbill

103. *Rutaceae* Rue Family
   Zanthoxylum clava-herculis – Hercules'-club, prickly ash, toothache tree

106. *Polygalaceae* Milkwort Family
   Polygala cymosa – tall milkwort
   Polygala lutea – yellow milkwort, candy weed

107. *Euphorbiaceae* Spurge Family
   Cnidoscolus stimulosus – bull-nettle
   Croton glandulosus var. *septentrionalis* – croton
   Croton punctatus – seaside croton
   Euphorbia heterophylla – poinsettia[n]
   Euphorbia ipecacuanhae – Carolina ipecac
   Euphorbia polygonifolia – seaside or beach spurge

110. *Anacardiaceae* Cashew Family
   Rhus copallina – dwarf or winged sumac
   Rhus radicans – poison ivy

112. *Aquifoliaceae* Holly Family
   Ilex cassine – dahoon, cassena
   Ilex glabra – inkberry, bitter gallberry
   Ilex opaca – American holly
   Ilex vomitoria – yaupon

113. *Celastraceae* Staff-Tree Family
   Euonymus americanus – strawberry bush

115. *Aceraceae* Maple Family
   Acer rubrum – red maple

119. *Rhamnaceae* Buckthorn Family
   Berchemia scandens – rattan-vine, supple jack

120. *Vitaceae* Vine Family
   Ampelopsis arborea – pepper-vine
   Parthenocissus quinquefolia – Virginia creeper
   Vitis aestivalis – summer or pigeon grape
   Vitis rotundifolia – muscadine grape, scuppernong

122. *Malvaceae* Mallow Family
   Hibiscus moscheutos – swamp rose mallow
   Kosteletskya virginica – seashore mallow
   Sida rhombifolia

Herbarium List 145

126. *Hypericaceae* St. John's-wort Family
 Hypericum cistifolium
 Hypericum drummondii – St. John's-wort[n]
 Hypericum gentianoides – pineweed, orange grass
 Hypericum hypericoides – St. Andrew's cross
 Hypericum mutilum – dwarf St. John's-wort
 Hypericum perfortum – St. John's-wort[n]
 Hypericum walteri – St. John's-wort[n]

129. *Cistaceae* Rockrose Family
 Helianthemum canadense – frostweed, rockrose
 Hudsonia tomentosa – beach heather, woolly hudsonia
 Lechea villosa – pin weed

130. *Violaceae* Violet Family
 Viola emarginata – triangle-leaf violet[n]
 Viola papilionacea – confederate violet
 Viola primulifolia – primrose-leaf violet[n]
 Viola rafinesquii – wild pansy

131. *Passifloraceae* Passion-Flower Family
 Passiflora incarnata – maypops, passion-flower
 Passiflora lutea – passion-flower, yellow passion-flower

132. *Cactaceae* Cactus Family
 Opuntia compressa – cactus, prickly pear
 Opuntia drummondii – prickly pear, cactus, Indian fig

134. *Elaeagnaceae* Oleaster Family
 Eleagnus pungens – silver berry[n]

135. *Lythraceae* Loosestrife Family
 Decodon verticillatus – water loosestrife, water willow
 Lythrum lineare – loosestrife, linear-leaved loosestrife

136. *Melastomataceae* Meadow-Beauty Family
 Rhexia alifanus – Savannah meadow-beauty[n]
 Rhexia mariana – Maryland meadow-beauty
 Rhexia virginica[n]

137. *Onagraceae* Evening Primrose Family
 Gaura angustifolia
 Ludwigia alternifolia – seedbox[n]
 Ludwigia maritima
 Oenothera biennis – common evening primrose[n]
 Oenothera fruticosa – sundrops
 Oenothera humifusa – beach evening primrose, seaside evening primrose
 Oenothera laciniata – evening primrose
 Oenothera laciniata var. *grandiflora* – evening primrose

Oenothera speciosa—sundrops, showy evening primrose[n]
Oenothera tetragona—sundrops[n]

138. Haloragaceae Water-Milfoil Family
Myriophyllum exalbescens—water-milfoil[n]
Prosperpinaca palustris—mermaid weed

139. Araliaceae Ginseng Family
Aralia spinosa—Hercules'-club
Hedera helix—English ivy

140. Apiaceae Parsley Family
Apium leptophyllum—marsh parsley[n]
Centella asiatica
Chaerophyllum tainturieri—wild chervil[n]
Cicuta maculata—spotted water-hemlock
Daucus carota—Queen Anne's lace, wild carrot[n]
Eryngium aquaticum—rattlesnake-master
Eryngium maritimum—beach or sea holly
Hydrocotyle bonariensis—seaside pennywort, large leaf pennywort
Hydrocotyle ranunculoides—water pennywort
Ptilimnium capillaceum—mock bishop's-weed
Sanicula marilandica—black snakeroot[n]

141. Nyssaceae Sour-Gum Family
Nyssa sylvatica—black gum

142. Cornaceae Dogwood Family
Cornus florida—flowering dogwood
Cornus stricta—swamp dogwood

143. Clethraceae White Alder Family
Clethra alnifolia—coast pepperbush, white alder

145. Ericaceae Heath Family
Chimaphila maculata—spotted pipsissewa
Chimaphila umbellata—spotted pipsissewa[n]
Gaylussacia frondosa—dangleberry
Kalmia angustifolia var. caroliniana—sheep laurel
Lyonia ligustrina—maleberry, male-blueberry
Lyonia lucida—fetter-bush
Monotropa uniflora—Indian pipe, corpse-plant
Rhododendron atlanticum—dwarf azalea
Vaccinium arboreum—tree sparkleberry
Vaccinium atrococcum—black highbush huckleberry
Vaccinium macrocarpon—cranberry
Vaccinium stamineum—squaw-huckleberry, gooseberry

147. *Primulaceae* Primrose Family
Hottonia inflata—water violet
Samolus parviflorus—water pimpernel

148. *Plumbaginaceae* Leadwort Family
Limonium carolinianum—sea lavender, marsh rosemary

150. *Ebenaceae* Ebony Family
Diospyros virginiana—persimmon[n]

153. *Oleaceae* Olive Family
Ligustrum sinense—privet
Osmanthus americanus—wild olive, devilwood

154. *Loganiaceae* Logania Family
Cynoctonum mitreola—miterwort
Gelsemium sempervirens—yellow or Carolina jessamine
Polypremum procumbens

155. *Gentianaceae* Gentian Family
Sabatia angularis—rose pink, bitter-bloom[n]
Sabatia campanulata—marsh pink
Sabatia dodecandra—large marsh pink, sea-pink
Sabatia stellaris—marsh pink, sea-pink

156. *Apocynaceae* Dogbane Family
Apocynum cannabinum—Indian hemp

157. *Asclepiadaceae* Milkweed Family
Asclepias amplexicaulis—curly milkweed
Asclepias incarnata ssp. *pulchre*—swamp milkweed
Asclepias lanceolata—marsh milkweed
Asclepias longifolia
Asclepias syriaca—common milkweed[n]
Asclepias tuberosa—butterfly-weed, pleurisy-root
Asclepias variegata—variegated milkweed
Cynanchum palustre

158. *Convolvulaceae* Morning Glory Family
Bonamia humistrata—trailing morning glory
Calystegia soldanella—beach morning glory
Cuscuta gronovii—dodder
Ipomoea pandurata—wild potato-vine[n]
Ipomoea purpurea—common morning glory[n]
Ipomoea sagittata—arrowleaf or seaside morning glory

159. *Polemoniaceae* Polemonium Family
Phlox drummondii—annual phlox
Phlox pilosa—phlox[n]

161. *Boraginaceae* Borage Family
Echium vulgare – viper's bugloss[n]

162. *Verbenaceae* Vervain Family
Callicarpa americana – French mulberry, beauty-berry
Lippia lanceolata – frogbit
Lippia nodiflora – fog-fruit, frogbit

164. *Lamiaceae* Mint Family
Lamium amplexicaule – henbit
Mentha piperita – peppermint
Monarda punctata – dotted horsemint
Salvia lyrata – lyre-leaved sage[n]
Scutellaria integrifolia – hyssop skullcap
Scutellaria integrifolia var. *hispidia* – hyssop skullcap
Stachys hyssopifolia var. *ambigua* – hyssop skullcap[n]
Teucrium canadense – wood-sage
Trichostema dichotomum – bluecurls

165. *Solanaceae* Nightshade Family
Datura stramonium – jimson weed
Physalis viscosa ssp. *maritima* – maritime ground-cherry, husk tomato
Solanum carolinense – nightshade, horse-nettle
Solanum nigrum – nightshade

166. *Scrophulariaceae* Figwort Family
Agalinis maritima – gerardia, seaside foxglove
Agalinis purpurea – gerardia, false foxglove
Aureolaria flava – false foxglove[n]
Bacopa monnieri – water-hyssop
Linaria canadensis – blue or old-field toadflax
Verbascum blattaria – moth mullein
Verbascum thapsus – woolly mullein

167. *Bignoniaceae* Bignonia Family
Anisostichus capreolata – cross-vine[n]
Campsis radicans – cow-itch, trumpet vine or creeper

169. *Orobanchaceae* Broom-Rape Family
Conopholis americana – squaw-root, cancer-root[n]

170. *Lentibulariaceae* Bladderwort Family
Utricularia inflata – bladderwort[n]
Utricularia subulata – bladderwort

171. *Acanthaceae* Acanthus Family
Ruellia caroliniensis – hairy ruellia[n]

172. *Plantaginaceae* Plantain Family
Plantago aristata – plantain, bracted plantain

Plantago indica – plantain[ns]
Plantago lanceolata – English plantain
Plantago major – common plantain
Plantago virginica – hoary plantain, dwarf plantain

173. *Rubiaceae* Madder Family
Cephalanthus occidentalis – button bush[n]
Diodia teres – buttonweed
Diodia virginiana – buttonweed
Galium boreale – northern bedstraw[ns]
Galium pilosum – bedstraw
Galium tinctorium – bedstraw
Mitchella repens – partridge berry

174. *Caprifoliaceae* Honeysuckle Family
Lonicera japonica – Japanese honeysuckle
Lonicera sempervirens – coral or trumpet honeysuckle
Sambucus canadensis – elderberry
Viburnum rufidulum – southern black-haw, blue haw[n]

175. *Valerianaceae* Valerian Family
Valerianella radiata – corn-salad

177. *Cucurbitaceae* Gourd Family
Melothria pendula – creeping cucumber

178. *Campanulaceae* Bluebell Family
Lobelia cardinalis – cardinal flower
Lobelia elongata – longleaf lobelia
Lobelia nuttallii – Nuttall's lobelia
Specularia perfoliata – Venus' looking-glass

179. *Asteraceae* Aster or Composite Family
Achillea millefolium – common yarrow, milfoil
Ambrosia artemisiifolia – common ragweed
Aster dumosus – bushy aster
Aster ericoides – heath aster[ns]
Aster patens
Aster racemosus – stalked flower aster[n]
Aster subulatus – seaside aster
Aster tenuifolius – slender-leaved aster
Aster tortifolius
Baccharis halimifolia – groundsel-tree, sea-myrtle, salt myrtle
Bidens bipinnata – Spanish needles[n]
Bidens laevis – wild-goldenglow
Bidens mitis
Borrichia frutescens – sea ox-eye

Carduus spinosissimus – yellow thistle, spiny thistle
Carphephorus bellidifolius[n]
Carphephorus tomentosus
Chrysanthemum leucanthemum – ox-eye daisy, white daisy
Cichorium intybus – common chicory, blue sailors[n]
Cirsium spinosissimus – yellow thistle[n]
Coreopsis angustifolia
Coreopsis basalis – calliopsis[n]
Coreopsis falcata
Coreopsis lanceolata – lance-leaved coreopsis
Crepis japonica – hawk's-beard[n]
Elephantopus tomentosus – elephant's foot
Erechtites hieracifolia – fireweed
Erigeron annuus – daisy fleabane[n]
Erigeron canadensis var. *canadensis* – horseweed, hogweed
Erigeron canadensis var. *pusillus* – horseweed, hogweed
Erigeron philadelphicus – common fleabane, daisy fleabane[n]
Erigeron quercifolius – daisy fleabane
Erigeron strigosus – narrow-leaved daisy fleabane[n]
Erigeron vernus – Robin's plantain
Eupatorium album – white thoroughwort
Eupatorium capillifolium – dog fennel, yankee weed
Eupatorium coelestinum – ageratum, mistflower[n]
Eupatorium cuneifolium
Eupatorium hyssopifolium – hyssop-leaved thoroughwort
Eupatorium recurvans
Eupatorium rotundifolium – round-leaved thoroughwort
Eupatorium serotinum – late-flowering thoroughwort
Gaillardia pulchella – gaillardia, blanket flower
Gnaphalium chilense – everlasting
Gnaphalium obtusifolium – rabbit tobacco
Gnaphalium purpureum – cudweed, everlasting
Helenium amarum – bitter-weed, sneezeweed
Helenium autumnale – common autumn sneezeweed, swamp sunflower[n]
Helianthus annuus – common sunflower
Heterotheca gossypina – duney aster, decumbent golden aster
Heterotheca nervosa var. *nervosa*
Heterotheca subaxillaris – camphorweed
Hieracium gronovii – hawkweed
Hypochaeris glabra – cat's ear
Hypochaeris radicata – cat's ear
Iva frutescens – shrubby marsh elder
Iva imbricata – marsh elder, seaside elder
Krigia virginica – dwarf dandelion

Lactuca canadensis—wild lettuce
Liatris graminifolia—blazing star[n]
Mikania scandens—climbing hempweed, boneset
Pluchea foetida—marsh fleabane
Pluchea purpurascens—camphorweed, salt-marsh fleabane
Prenanthes serpentaria—gall-of-the-earth, lion's-foot
Pyrrhopappus carolinianus—false dandelion, fireweed
Senecio tomentosus—woolly ragwort[n]
Solidago erecta—slender goldenrod
Solidago fistulosa—pine-barren goldenrod
Solidago graminifolia—lance-leaved goldenrod[n]
Solidago microcephala—bush goldenrod
Solidago puberula—downy goldenrod[n]
Solidago puberula var. *pulverulenta*[n]
Solidago sempervirens var. *mexicana*—seaside goldenrod
Solidago stricta
Solidago tenuifolia—slender fragrant goldenrod
Sonchus asper—spiny-leaved sow-thistle
Taraxacum officinale—common dandelion
Xanthium strumarium—cocklebur

Reference List

Bianchini, F., and Corbetta, F. *Health Plants of the World*. New York: Newsweek Books, 1977.

Boyce, Oleta Merry. *Plant Uses by New Mexico's Early Natives*. Santa Fe, N.M.: Rydal Press, 1974.

Duncan, Wilbur H., and Foote, Leonard E. *Wildflowers of the Southeastern United States*. Athens: University of Georgia Press, 1975.

Fernald, Merrit L. *Gray's Manual of Botany*. 8th ed. New York: D. Van Nostrand, 1950.

Foley, Daniel J. *Gardening by the Sea*. Philadelphia: Chilton, 1965.

Graetz, Karl E. *Seacoast Plants of the Carolinas*. Raleigh: U.S. Department of Agriculture, Soil Conservation Service, 1973.

Grimm, William Carey. *Recognizing Flowering Wild Plants*. New York: Hawthorn, 1968.

Hardin, J. W., and Arena, J. M. *Human Poisoning from Native and Cultivated Plants*. 2nd ed. Durham: Duke University Press, 1974.

Hardin, James W., and Committee. "Vascular Plants." *Endangered and Threatened Plants and Animals of North Carolina*, edited by John E. Cooper, Sarah S. Robinson, and John B. Funderburg. Raleigh: North Carolina State Museum of Natural History, 1977.

Hariot, Thomas. *A Briefe and True Report of the New Found Land of Virginia*. Murfreesboro, N.C.: Johnson Publishing, 1969.

House, Homer D. *Wildflowers*. New York: Macmillan Company, 1942.

Justice, William S., and Bell, C. Ritchie. *Wildflowers of North Carolina*. Chapel Hill: University of North Carolina Press, 1968.

Krochmal, Arnold, and Krochmal, Connie. *A Guide to Medicinal Plants of the U.S.* Chicago: Quadrangle, 1973.

Kuijt, Job. *Common Coulee Plants of Southern Alberta*. Lethbridge, Alta.: University of Lethbridge, Productive Service, 1972.

Lorant, Stefan. *The New World*. New York: Duell, Sloan and Pearce, 1946.

Morton, Julia. *Folk Remedies of the Low Country*. Miami: E. A. Seemann, 1974.

Olsen, Larry Dean. *Outdoor Survival Skills*. Provo: Brigham Young University Press, 1976.

Peterson, Roger Tory, and McKenny, Margaret. *Field Guide to Wild Flowers of Northeastern and Northcentral North America*. Boston: Houghton Mifflin, 1968.

Petrides, George A. *A Field Guide to Trees and Shrubs*. Boston: Houghton Mifflin, 1972.

Preston, Richard J., Jr., and Wright, Valerie G. *Identification of South-eastern Trees in Winter*. Raleigh: North Carolina Agricultural Extension Service, 1976.

Radford, Albert E.; Ahles, Harry E.; and Bell, C. Ritchie. *Manual of the Vascular Flora of the Carolinas*. Chapel Hill: University of North Carolina Press, 1968.

Reed, Chester A. *The Flower Guide—Wildflowers East of the Rockies*. New York: Doubleday, Page & Company, 1916.

Rickett, H. W., and Grehan, Farrell. *American Wildflowers*. New York: Odyssey, 1964.

Rogers, Julia Ellen. *The Tree Guide—Trees East of the Rockies*. New York: Doubleday, Page & Company, 1916.

Schetky, EthelJane McD., and Woodward, Carol H. "The Ageless Art of Dyeing." In *Dye Plants and Dyeing—A Handbook* (special printing of *Plants and Gardens*, vols. 20, no. 3). Baltimore: Brooklyn Botanic Garden, 1964.

Sweet, Muriel. *Common Edible and Useful Plants of the West*. Healdsburg, Ca.: Naturegraph Publishers, 1976.

Rare and Endangered Species

For various reasons, some plant species are rare in North Carolina. They may be at the periphery of their ranges or they may be long-range disjuncts or endemics. They are considered as either endangered or threatened by the very fact that they are rare and in some danger of becoming extinct.

North Carolina, especially the Outer Banks, has many plants that are at their farthest northern or southern distribution. A peripheral species may be very common outside of North Carolina, but rare here at the limit of its distribution.

The endemics, long-range disjuncts, and those species that are rare throughout the country are of greater concern. Endemic applies to a species confined or indigenous to a certain small area. Such a species exists nowhere else in the world, except possibly under cultivation. A long-range disjunct is a rare segment of a species population, separated by a few hundred miles or more from its main area of distribution, where it may be quite common. Such populations are often relics of past geological times. They usually mark a unique and interesting habitat within the state, worthy of preservation.

Reference is often made to plants as common or uncommon or as frequent or infrequent in an area. However, frequency can change from year to year, depending on drought (level of water table), storms (intrusion of salt water), wind (damage from sand blast, high evaporation, or salt spray), temperature range (exceedingly high summer temperatures can weaken or kill a northern-type plant, and an overnight drop in temperature from 60° to 6° can damage many hardy plants and surely kill the southern-type perennial or shrub).

Glossary

Annual. *A plant that grows from seed to fruit in one year, then dies.*
Anther. *The pollen-bearing or fertile part of the stamen.*
Aquatic. *A plant living in water part or all of its life cycle.*
Axil. *The angle between the stem and a leaf.*
Basal. *Situated at or growing from the base of the stem.*
Biennial. *A plant which completes its life cycle and dies naturally in two years.*
Brackish. *Salty, as water in saline soil; or, as fresh water where tides or wind introduce salt water.*
Bract. *A reduced or modified leaf, usually at the base of a flower.*
Bud. *An undeveloped shoot or stem; an unexpanded flower.*
Calyx. *The outer set of leafy parts of a flower; collective name for sepals.*
Catkin. *A scaly, spikelike cluster of inconspicuous flowers, usually either male or female.*
Cluster. *Flowers borne not singly, but in a variety of combinations.*
Colony. *A stand, group, or population of plants of one species.*
Composite flowers. *The centers are clusters of many disc flowers, often, as in asters and daisies, surrounded by a circle of ray flowers.*
Corm. *The enlarged fleshy base of a stem, bulblike but solid.*
Corolla. *The inner set of leafy parts of a flower; collective name for petals.*
Corymb. *A flattopped or rounded cluster of flowers; the outer flowers open first.*
Crown. *An inner petallike appendage, as in narcissus.*
Decumbent. *Prostrate, but with the end of each branch pointed upward.*
Disc flower. *The tiny tubular flowers in the centers of the heads of composite flowers like asters and daisies.*
Dissected. *Cut or divided into numerous narrow segments.*
Endangered. *Threatened with extinction.*
Endemic. *A species geographically confined to a single limited area.*
Entire. *A leaf with smooth edges, without teeth or lobes.*
Epiphyte. *A plant that grows on another plant, but is not parasitic; an air-plant.*
Escaped from cultivation. *A plant that has escaped from cultivation and thrives in the wild.*
Family. *A major subdivision in the classification of plants.*
Fruit. *The seed-bearing product of a plant; a ripened ovary.*
Genus. *A subdivision of a family, usually including more than one species.*
Head. *A rounded or flattened cluster of stemless flowers.*
Herb. *A plant with no persistent woody stem above ground; a plant that is often used in seasoning and medicine.*

157

Herbaceous. *Plant parts that have little or no hard woody tissue and that die back in the winter.*

Herbarium. *A collection of pressed plant specimens, prepared for permanent preservation and arranged systematically.*

Hirsute. *With moderate coarse or stiff hairs.*

Hoary. *Covered with short white or gray hairs.*

Hummocks. *Small rounded hills.*

Introduced. *Brought from another region; not native to the region where found.*

Lagoon. *A shallow pond, sound, or lake, especially one near or connected with the sea.*

Lobed. *Shallowly or deeply cut, resulting in rounded or pointed segments.*

Marsh. *An area normally covered with water year round.*

Native. *Originating in a particular place, region, country.*

Node. *A section of stem from which leaves or branches grow.*

Nutlet. *A hard, one-seeded fruit smaller than a nut.*

Palmate. *A leaf that is lobed, divided, or ribbed in a palmlike or handlike fashion.*

Parasite. *A plant growing upon and obtaining nourishment from another living organism.*

Perennial. *A plant that lives three or more years.*

Petal. *The inner leafy part of a flower, usually white or colorful.*

Pinnate. *A compound leaf with leaflets arranged on either side of a common axis; featherlike.*

Pistil. *The female organ of a flower comprising the ovary, style, and stigma.*

Prostrate. *A general term for lying flat on ground.*

Pubescent. *Covered with soft, short hairs.*

Ray. *Flattened petallike corolla at the periphery of composite flowers, such as asters and daisies; or one of a number of stems radiating from a common center—as in an umbel.*

Rayless. *Having no raylike parts.*

Rhizome. *Any prostrate underground stem.*

Rose hip. *Rose fruit; ripened ovary of a rose.*

Salt marsh. *Flat land subject to overflow by salt water.*

Salt-resistant. *Able to withstand or tolerate salt in spray and salt-laden wind.*

Savannah. *Grassland containing scattered trees and drought-resistant undergrowth.*

Sepal. *A part of the calyx, the outer parts of a flower.*

Serrate. *Having sharp teeth pointing forward.*

Short-lived perennial. *Plant may not live more than three years.*

Shrub. *Woody perennial, usually branching from the base with several main stems.*

Sound. *Long passage of water connecting two larger bodies of water or forming a channel between the mainland and an island; wider and more extensive than a strait.*

Spathe. *A leaflike sheath partly enclosing a stem or flower.*
Species. *A subdivision of a genus; includes related individuals that resemble one another.*
Spine. *Sharp-pointed woody or rigid outgrowth on a plant; thorn.*
Spiral. *Winding, coiling, or circling around a stem.*
Stamen. *The pollen-producing organ of a flower comprising anther and filament.*
Stigma. *The tip of the pistil.*
Stipules. *Basal paired appendages of a leaf, sometimes fused.*
Style. *Part of the pistil, between ovary and stigma.*
Succulent. *Juicy, fleshy.*
Thicket. *Dense growth of shrubbery.*
Tree. *Perennial woody plant of considerable stature with a single trunk.*
Tuber. *Thickened subterranean stem, typically with numerous buds—for example, potato.*
Umbel. *A flower cluster in which the stems arise from the same point.*
Variegated. *Diversified exterior colors; dappled appearance.*
Winter annual. *An annual plant that lives through the winter and flowers in late winter or early spring.*
Whorl. *An arrangement of 3 or more leaves or flowers in a circle around the stem.*
Woolly. *Clothed with long or matted hairs.*

Index

Date Due